PRENTICE HALL
LITERATURE

PENGUIN EDITION

General Resources

Grade Six

PEARSON

Prentice Hall

Upper Saddle River, New Jersey
Boston, Massachusetts

ISBN 0-13-165103-X

2 3 4 5 6 7 8 9 10   10 09 08 07 06

Contents

PROFESSIONAL DEVELOPMENT 1

Differentiated Instruction 2

Vocabulary Knowledge Rating 4

Vocabulary Knowledge Rating Chart 5

Introducing Expressive Vocabulary 6

Anticipation Guide 8

Anticipation Guide Form 10

KWL 11

KWL Chart 12

Vocab-o-Gram 13

Vocab-o-Gram Chart 14

Word Forms 15

Word Form Chart 16

Response Journals 17

Response Journal Starters .19

Two-Column Response Journal 20

Literature Circles 21

Roles in Literature Circles 23

Save the Last Word for Me .24

Save the Last Word for Me Response Page 26

ReQuest (Reciprocal Questioning) 27

Question-Answer Relationships (QAR) 28

Reading Log 29

Reading Log, Student Page .30

Interpretation Chart 31

Interpretation Chart, Student Page 32

Paired Discussion 33

Paired Discussion, Student Page 34

Think-Write-Pair-Share 35

Think-Write-Pair-Share, Student Page 36

Give One, Get One 37

Give One, Get One, Student Page 38

Discussion Guide 39

WRITING RUBRICS FOR SELF-ASSESSMENT

LISTENING AND SPEAKING RUBRICS 41

Descriptive Essay *4-point, 5-point* 43

Descriptive Essay *6-point* .44

Autobiographical Narrative *4-point, 5-point* 45

Autobiographical Narrative *6-point* 46
Response to Literature *4-point, 5-point* 47
Response to Literature *6-point* 48
Short Story *4-point, 5-point* 49
Short Story *6-point* 50
How-to Essay *4-point, 5-point* 51
How-to Essay *6-point* 52
Persuasive Essay *4-point, 5-point* 53
Persuasive Essay *6-point* 54
Writing for Assessment Essay *4-point, 5-point* .55
Writing for Assessment Essay *6-point* 56
Comparison-and-Contrast Essay *4-point, 5-point* 57
Comparison-and-Contrast Essay *6-point* 58
Letter *4-point, 5-point* 59
Letter *6-point* 60
Cause-and-Effect Essay *4-point, 5-point* 61
Cause-and-Effect Essay *6-point* 62
Multimedia Report *4-point, 5-point* 63
Multimedia Report *6-point* 64
Research Report *4-point, 5-point* 65
Research Report *6-point* 66
Problem-Solution Essay *4-point, 5-point* 67
Problem-Solution Essay *6-point* 68
Summary *4-point, 5-point* 69
Summary *6-point* 70
Poem (Rhyming) *4-point, 5-point* 71
Poem (Rhyming) *6-point* 72
Critique *4-point, 5-point* 73
Critique *6-point* 74
Biography *4-point, 5-point* 75
Biography *6-point* 76
Reader Response Journal *4-point, 5-point* 77
Reader Response Journal *6-point* 78
Generic (Holistic) Writing Rubric *4-point, 5-point* 79
Generic (Holistic) Writing Rubric *6-point* 80
Listening: Evaluating a Persuasive Presentation 81
Listening: Analyzing Media Messages 82
Listening: Evaluating Advertisements 83
Listening: Evaluating a Media Presentation 84

General Resources

Listening and Speaking: Giving and Receiving Oral Directions 85

Speaking: Narrative Account 86

Speaking: Presenting a Proposal 87

Speaking: Organizing and Delivering an Oral Summary 88

Speaking: Delivering a Research Presentation 89

Speaking: Presenting Pros and Cons 90

ALTERNATIVE ASSESSMENT MATERIALS 91

Reading Strategy Inventory 93

Preparing to Read 96

Independent Reading Guide: The Novel 98

Independent Reading Guide: The Short Story 100

Independent Reading Guide: The Play 102

Independent Reading Guide: Nonfiction 104

Independent Reading Guide: Poetry 106

Independent Reading Guide: Myths and Folk Tales 108

Initial Self-Assessment: Writing 110

Peer Conferencing Notes: Reader 112

Proofreading Checklist 114

Writing Self-Assessment 116

Portfolio Planner 118

Portfolio Record 120

Portfolio Final Self-Evaluation 122

Portfolio Final Evaluation: Teacher Rating 123

Self-Assessment: Speech 125

Peer Assessment: Speech 126

Peer Assessment: Oral Interpretation 127

Peer Assessment: Dramatic Performance 128

Self-Assessment: Listening 129

Self-Assessment: Speaking and Listening Progress 130

Speaking Progress Chart: Teacher Observation 131

Teacher Observation Checklist 132

Home Parent Letter 135

Self-Assessment Home Review 136

Homework Log 137

Writing: Home Review Letter 138

Professional Development

Differentiated Instruction

Description

The wide range of academic diversity found in schools today presents both a challenge and an opportunity to all teachers. The goal of a comprehensive language arts program remains the provision of universal access for all students to an intellectually rich and challenging language arts curriculum and instruction in addition to whatever specialized intervention may be required.

Universal access occurs when teachers provide curriculum and instruction in ways that allow all learners in the classroom to participate and to achieve the instructional and behavioral goals of general education and the core curriculum. Teachers will succeed in providing universal access if they teach in heterogeneous, inclusive classrooms and consistently and systematically integrate instructional strategies that are responsive to the needs of typical learners, gifted learners, less proficient readers, English language learners, and students who are eligible for and receiving special education services.

Strategies

The following is a basic list of instructional considerations that can be applied across all phases of instruction.

- **Clarify behavioral expectations** for the lesson. Students need to understand the parameters within which they are working.

- **Provide time for students to collect their thoughts** before having to speak. You may want to ask a student a question and then pause before you assist the student in responding. You may also want to ask the student a question, state that you want the student to think about it, and indicate that you will be back for the response in a minute. Another possibility is to tell students the questions that you will be asking during tomorrow's class in order to give them time, overnight, to prepare their responses. These suggestions can be very helpful for a student experiencing a language disability or for a student who uses an alternative, augmentative communication device.

- **Use visuals throughout the lesson.** Outlining key ideas, writing key phrases and vocabulary on the overhead projector or board, or putting notes on the overhead projector or board are critical supports for many students. You may want to provide some students with a copy of your overheads or notes ahead of time so that they can follow along. For other students, make a partial or blank copy of the graphic or outline you will be using and require students to write in key information as it is discussed. It is very helpful if you model this filling-in procedure for students. It also helps them to overcome problems with spelling or capturing complex ideas using only a few words.

- **Schedule opportunities for preteaching and reteaching** key concepts, vocabulary words, and skills. Students will most likely need more than one opportunity to gain understanding and fluency.

- **Assist in time management.** When requiring students to complete projects or long-term assignments, provide a calendar that breaks down the requirements by due dates. Go over the checklist with the students and monitor their use of the checklist and task completion as the assignment proceeds. Many students will experience significant difficulties in self-managing the time needed to complete complex and long-term assignments.

- **Consider alternative means for demonstrating understanding.** Think beyond the common modes of reading and writing. Students could present information orally, create a poster or visual representation of a work, tape-record their ideas, or act out their understanding. These activities take into consideration multiple intelligences and can provide access for all learners in the classroom.

- **Have students begin all work in class.** Prior to class dismissal, check to ensure that each student has a good start and understands what is expected.

- **Build vocabulary** by teaching the meaning of prefixes and suffixes. Also, focus on synonyms and antonyms of words and have students define the words in their own words.

- **Explicitly teach note-taking skills.** Model note-taking as you present information to the classroom. Collect and review the students' notes and provide suggestions for improvement.

- **Use recorded readings.** Some students can benefit from the use of books on tape/CD. Be sure that students are actively engaged and following along as they listen to the tape/CD.

- **Balance student-focused and directed activities with teacher-focused and directed activities.** Students who are less proficient readers, English language learners, and students with disabilities will often require explicit instruction and modeling. Student-focused activities may assist students in gaining numerous skills, but they need to be balanced with teacher-directed lessons that provide explicit instruction by the teacher. Clearly stating expectations, modeling what students are to do, providing examples of finished projects, and explicitly teaching vocabulary words, reading comprehension strategies, and strategies for approaching text in a strategic, active way are necessary for these students' success. Other students can benefit from this explicitness of instruction as well. Being explicit does not mean watering down or dumbing down the curriculum; it means making it explicit so that all students can access it.

Vocabulary Knowledge Rating

Description

Vocabulary Knowledge Rating is a strategy for assessing students' familiarity with important terms in a reading selection by having them independently rate how well they know these terms. This preassessment enables you to get a realistic gauge of students' expressive and receptive vocabulary knowledge—that is, words they actually understand versus words they simply recognize. You are then able to provide focused and substantive preteaching as necessary.

Steps

1. List the Vocabulary Builder words and expressive vocabulary for a given selection on a Vocabulary Knowledge Rating Chart and distribute copies of it. When students have the list, tell them that they will prepare for reading the new selection by assessing what they already know about important vocabulary in it.

2. Pronounce each word as students complete the knowledge-rating process so that decoding is not a problem. As you read each word aloud, ask students to rate their word knowledge by checking one of the columns on the chart:

   1 = Know it: I know this word well (can define it and use it in an intelligent sentence).
   2 = Kind of know it: I have heard or seen this word (but not sure what it means).
   3 = Do not know it: I have not seen or heard the word before.

   Remind students not to indicate that they *know* a word (Rating 1) if they simply *recognize* a word (Rating 2). Also encourage them not to hesitate to indicate that they do not recognize or understand a word at all (Rating 3). Invite them to be honest, as you will use their input to decide what words you will preteach and discuss.

3. Use the ratings for a unified-class discussion. Tally how many students actually know (or think they know) each word and encourage them to share their knowledge. In this way, you will be able to gauge just how much prereading instruction you need to provide. Follow up this assessment and brainstorming process with focused instruction of terms that are totally unfamiliar, somewhat familiar, or clearly misunderstood.

4. Draw students' attention to the Vocabulary Builder notations in the side columns of their textbook. Point out that the words are placed to provide them with a meaning in the context of the reading. They should apply the meanings as they read.

5. After you have completed instruction and students have read the assigned selection, have them return to their Vocabulary Knowledge Rating Charts and re-rate themselves. Then, return to the selection or use reference books to clarify words that are still problematic.

6. Let students know that this Vocabulary Knowledge Rating Chart is an organizer for study. Any words on the list may appear on the Selection Test. Students should also be held accountable for using these terms in related oral or written work.

Source

Blachowicz, C., and Fisher, P.J. (2002). *Teaching Vocabulary in All Classrooms.* Upper Saddle River, NJ: Merrill/Prentice Hall.

Vocabulary Knowledge Rating Chart

Directions: As your teacher reads the words, think about what each word might mean and mark the appropriate number in the Before Reading column.

① = Know it　　② = Kind of know it　　③ = Do not know it

After you have read and discussed the selection, rate the words again in the After Reading column. Then, write definitions and examples or sentences to help you clarify and remember the words.

Selection _____

Word	Rating		Definition	Example/Sentence
	Before Reading	After Reading		

Introducing Expressive Vocabulary

Background

Vocabulary is the term we use to describe the total number of words and phrases an individual understands at some level. Language researchers often describe vocabulary being further subdivided into receptive vocabulary, which are words understood from listening or reading, and expressive vocabulary, which are words communicated by speaking or writing. Receptive or passive vocabulary is typically far larger than expressive vocabulary, including many words that are at least partially understood but not fully integrated into one's expressive vocabulary. To succeed academically, students need to not only recognize a wide array of specialized terminology, but also comfortably utilize sophisticated vocabulary in both oral and written contexts.

Instructional Implications

Research suggests that the comprehensive development of academic vocabulary, the particular terms used primarily in academic settings, requires directly teaching new terms (receptive vocabulary) and structured tasks that require students to apply newly acquired words in discussion and writing to build their expressive vocabulary. Unfortunately, simply listening to articulate language used by a teacher or encountering novel terms in a reading selection will not automatically transfer to confident and competent student application. Practical guidelines for introducing new terms as well as fostering expressive vocabulary development via structured discussion and writing tasks are provided in the following sections.

Steps to Teach a New Term

1. **Pronounce the word and clarify the part of speech.**
   This article focuses on an ecstatic moment in a high school student's life. Ecstatic is an adjective, a word used to describe.

2. **Ask students to all repeat the word once or twice.**
   Say the word ecstatic with me. (ec stat' ic)

3. **Explain—provide an accessible synonym and/or a brief explanation.**
   Ecstatic means extremely happy.

4. **Elaborate—make connections (image, descriptive sentence, etc.).**
   Showing image: a picture of a soccer team receiving the championship trophy.
   Showing sentence: I was ecstatic when our team won the soccer championship.

5. **Assess—Ask focused questions to see if students seem to grasp the word's meaning (vs. Any questions? Do you understand? Is that clear?).**
   Would you be ecstatic if you won the lottery?
   Would you be ecstatic if you were assigned a 20-page report to complete over Spring break?

Steps to Structuring the Expressive Use of a New Term

Simply telling students to use newly taught words in discussion and writing activities is not likely to significantly enhance expressive vocabulary. Students will be far more likely to independently use a richer variety of academic language if they have had the benefit of initial structured classroom application tasks.

Structured Oral Applications via Guided Writing and Discussion

Discussion:

1. **Review the target word.**
   "One of our target academic terms that means exceptionally happy is _____."
   (that is correct, ecstatic)

2. **Model the appropriate use of the new term in a complete sentence (with appropriate syntax and grammar).**
   "I was ecstatic to hear our team had won the championship."
   "I was ecstatic when I learned that our team had won the championship."

3. **Provide one or more sentence starters for students to complete individually**
   "I was ecstatic when_____."
   "I was ecstatic to_____."

4. **Partner rehearsal:** Students take turns sharing their examples using complete sentences including the target word.

5. **Class discussion:** Structured sharing of relevant examples, provide feedback and remodeling as necessary.

Writing:

Linguistic scaffolds such as sentence starters or paragraph frames are particularly helpful for less proficient writers; however, they are not meant to be straitjackets for students capable of more creative and autonomous application. Without structured applications, students most in need of developing academic discourse skills are apt to flounder, producing poorly constructed written products comprised largely of everyday spoken English.

1. **Design a task that warrants the application of the new vocabulary.**
   For example, sentences, paragraphs, and essays.
   #### Sentence Level
   Provide relevant sentence starters that model the appropriate use of the word as well as sentence structure (syntax and grammar).
   "I was ecstatic (base form of verb: e.g., to learn that_____, to receive_____, when I + verb/past tense)."
   #### Paragraph/Essay Level
   Provide a relevant sentence starter for each of the suggested terms.
   Provide a relevant paragraph frame including a topic sentence, transitional expressions, and target vocabulary.

2. **Assessment rubric**
   Use of target vocabulary is identified.
   For example, "The writer appropriately applies 4–6 new lesson terms."

Anticipation Guide

Description

A productive way to assess students' familiarity with a topic or concept and to motivate active and purposeful reading is to use an Anticipation Guide. The Anticipation Guide, initially developed by Herber (1978), enhances students' reading comprehension by activating their background knowledge and experiences, focusing their attention on the important concepts or big ideas addressed in the selection, and encourages them to react to specific ideas in the text. This strategy is appropriate for both narrative and informational texts.

Students react to thought-provoking statements on the Anticipation Guide before they read. An important element of strategy is the discussion that takes place after students independently respond to the statements. This prereading discussion of responses elicits relevant background knowledge, preconceived ideas, and any possible misconceptions. Because the Anticipation Guide revolves around the reading selection's most important concepts, students are motivated to pay close attention to this information while reading.

After reading the selection, students return to their prereading responses to see if the text actually supports their initial responses. You may have students identify evidence to support their postreading responses to the Anticipation Guide statements. When students have completed their reading and revisited their initial responses, you may use the Anticipation Guide to anchor the postreading discussion, enabling you to evaluate how well students have understood the material and to make sure that misconceptions have been corrected.

Steps

1. Using the form provided, create an Anticipation Guide for the selection students will read. You may insert the statements provided in the Motivation note in the Annotated Teacher's Edition, add further statements, or create your own statements.

   These statements should address key points, major concepts, and broad—possibly controversial—ideas students will encounter in the selection, rather than specific supporting details. They should be worded to provoke agreement or disagreement. The most effective statements are those about which students have some knowledge but do not necessarily have a complete or mature understanding. If appropriate, you might also include one or two statements that are likely to tap into glaring misconceptions about the topic. You might also consider planting a few important words from the selection or expressive vocabulary within your statements so that you have a focused opportunity to address them.

2. Copy the Anticipation Guide and distribute it to students. Read aloud each statement on the Anticipation Guide and clarify any potentially unfamiliar vocabulary. Tell students to react to each statement quietly and independently, formulate a response to it, and be prepared to defend their opinions.

3. If the ideas are fairly complex, place students with a partner or in small groups to discuss their reactions before debriefing as a unified class. They may indicate their consensus as a group in the "Group" column.

4. Engage the unified class in a prereading discussion by reading each statement aloud and then asking for a hand count (or thumbs up or down) of responses. Call on students from each side of the issue to justify their responses. Refrain from telling them the correct response, thereby negating any incentive to actually read the text.

5. Have students read the selection, with the purpose of finding evidence that confirms, rejects, or elaborates on each of the statements in the Anticipation Guide.

6. After students finish reading, have them return to the statements to determine whether they have changed their minds regarding any of the presented ideas. Either independently or in small groups, have them locate the information from the text that supports or disproves each statement. Students may then rewrite any statement that needs to be altered based on what they have read.

7. Lead a unified class discussion of what students have learned from the reading, tackling one statement at a time and asking students first to share relevant information from the text and then their revision (if necessary) of the original statement.

Sources

Buehl, D. (2001). *Classroom Strategies for Interactive Learning*. Newark, DE: International Reading Association.
Herber, H. (1978). *Teaching Reading in Content Areas*, 2nd ed. Upper Saddle River, NJ: Prentice Hall.
Readence, J.E., Bean, T.W., and Baldwin, R.S. (1995). *Content Area Reading: An Integrated Approach*, 5th ed. Dubuque, IA: Kendall/Hunt.
Wood, K.D. (2001). *Literacy Strategies Across the Subject Areas: Process-Oriented Blackline Masters for the K-12 Classroom*. Boston: Allyn and Bacon.

Name _____ Class_____ Date_____

Anticipation Guide Form

Directions: Before reading, mark in the Me column whether you agree (A) or disagree (D) with each statement. Be prepared to support your opinions with specific reasons and examples from your prior knowledge and experiences. Then, discuss your responses with your group and mark the group's decision in the Group column. As you read, look for information or details that support your opinion or cause you to change your mind. After reading, mark whether you still agree or disagree.

Selection _____

Before Reading		Statements	After Reading
Me	**Group**		
		1.	
		2.	
		3.	
		4.	
		5.	
		6.	
		7.	
		8.	

KWL

Description

KWL is a strategy that models the active thinking needed when getting ready to read and actually reading to learn from expository text. The letters *K, W,* and *L* stand for three activities students engage in when reading to learn: recalling what they *Know* (activating prior knowledge), determining what they *Want* to learn (setting a purpose for reading), and identifying what they *Learn* as they read (recalling and summarizing). It is a particularly useful strategy to apply to expository or informational texts. It is very important to scaffold the use of KWL with students. Do not just hand them the chart and expect them to use it on their own. Guide them through each phase of the process.

Steps

1. Engage students in a brainstorming session about what they as a group already know about the concept or the topic of the reading. Be aware that underprepared students may have little or no prior knowledge. In that case, it is important to engage in activities that clearly present the necessary background.

2. Students then write particular items they already know and particular items they want to know on individual KWL charts. You may further prepare them by eliciting their ideas about what types of information the reading selection should contain. For example, if the class is going to read an article on Cesar Chavez, students should be able to anticipate that there will be information about his family background, his experiences as a migrant farm worker and in union organizing, and some evaluation of his accomplishments. You may also provide additional items to guide students' reading or to emphasize important concepts.

3. After this preparation, students read the selection and jot down information they learn as they read. They look for information that answers their questions or adds to what they know.

4. When the reading is completed, the class discusses what they have learned, what questions have been answered, and what new questions have emerged. You may prompt them about new information that might not have been anticipated.

5. Finally, students organize and synthesize what they have learned—possibly in another graphic organizer—for study or for a possible writing assignment.

Sources

Buehl, D. (2001). *Classroom Strategies for Interactive Learning.* Newark, DE: International Reading Association.
Carr, E.M., and Ogle, D. (1987). "K-W-L Plus: A Strategy for Comprehension and Summarization." *Journal of Reading,* 28:626–631.

Name _____

Class _____ Date _____

KWL Chart

Directions: With your group, brainstorm and list **what you already Know** about _____ in the first column of the following chart. In the second column, write what you **Want to know** or find out from reading the selection. After you read, review your notes and record **what you Learned** in the third column of the chart.

Selection _____

What You Already *Know*	What You *Want* to Know	What You *Learned*

Vocab-o-Gram

Description

Vocab-o-Gram is a productive strategy for both comprehension and vocabulary. It is an appropriate strategy for use with fiction. A Vocab-o-Gram is a classification chart that includes the elements of story structure. Because students in middle grades and high school are familiar with story structure, if they are given some essential words, they can anticipate or predict what might be likely to happen.

Students are given selected words or phrases from a story and asked to organize them according to the story elements. The organized groups of words enable students to formulate ideas and make predictions about the story. After students read, they return to their Vocab-o-Gram charts and reevaluate their predictions and clarify vocabulary as necessary.

Steps

1. Select 10–20 words and phrases from a story that may reflect characters, setting, feelings, key ideas, or events. Present the words to students on the board or on an overhead.

2. Give students a copy of the Vocab-o-Gram chart. Have them work in pairs or small groups to share what they know about the words. They then decide which words give clues to the different elements of a story and place the words in the appropriate category on their charts. They may place words in more than one category.

3. Conduct a class discussion about students' placement of the words and their reasoning for the placement. Have students share their knowledge of words that may be unfamiliar.

4. After students have completed this discussion, they will have formed some preliminary ideas about the story. Have them state their preliminary ideas as predictions about the characters, events, and so on.

5. Suggest that each student also formulate one or two specific questions to answer.

6. After reading, return to the Vocab-o-Gram and refine their ideas. Review the vocabulary and clarify any words by returning to the selection or using reference works.

Source

Blachowicz, C., and Fisher, P.J. (2002). *Teaching Vocabulary in All Classrooms*. Upper Saddle River, NJ: Merrill/Prentice Hall.

Name _____ Class_____ Date _____

Vocab-o-Gram Chart

Directions: Insert the vocabulary in the categories in the first column where you think they might apply. Then, in the second column, make some predictions about the story elements based on the words you placed in the first column.

Selection _____

Words	Predictions
The setting	
The characters	
The problem or goal	
The actions or events	
The resolution	
Other	
What questions do you have?	
Unknown words	

Word Forms

Description

Students benefit from knowing related forms of words. Many of the Vocabulary Builder words with selections have important related forms. A Word Form Chart, similar to the one on the next page, is an excellent way to give students access to related word forms. This chart enables students to readily visualize vocabulary connections and to apply this new terminology in discussion of the selections and in follow-up writing tasks.

Steps

1. Determine which Vocabulary Builder words have other forms that are useful for students to know. Using the blank Word Form Chart provided, insert these new words in the appropriate category: *Noun, Verb, Adjective,* or *Adverb.* Not all words have forms for all parts of speech.

2. Distribute the chart to students and elicit from them any related word forms with which they may already be familiar. Then supply any critical unfamiliar forms. Refrain from supplying related word forms that are beyond the developmental range of your students. For example, when introducing the lesson term *prejudice* (noun) to a group of sixth-grade students with a high percentage of second-language learners and less-proficient readers, it would certainly be beneficial to point out the high-frequency adjective form *prejudiced* but inappropriate and overwhelming to dwell on the verb form *to prejudice,* which occurs mainly in legal contexts.

3. When assigning related word forms for students to identify, clarify the target parts of speech. For example, if you want them to identify only the adjective form of the noun *prejudice,* then place an asterisk in the adjective section on the Word Form Chart. This will prevent students from spinning their wheels trying to identify a part of speech that may not even exist or that may be out of their developmental range or beyond the assigned lesson topic.

4. Have students note that sometimes there are two forms of a particular part of speech. When this occurs, explain—or have students explain—the difference in meaning between the two word forms.

5. Encourage students to refer to their completed Word Form Charts when working on follow-up speaking and writing assignments. Hold them accountable for integrating new words in their speaking and writing and using the appropriate word form by factoring in the application of new vocabulary in your assessment practices, such as rubrics.

Name _____ Class _____ Date _____

Word Form Chart

Selection _____

Noun	Verb	Adjective	Adverb

Response Journals

Description

Response Journals can be set up in a number of ways and used for a variety of purposes. Response Journals are an opportunity for students to interact personally and independently with a piece of literature. Initially, students may be guided in their responses, with a Response Starters sheet, which provides a series of stems to be built into response statements. Later, students may work in a two-column response format, with prepared sheets or in their own notebooks.

Response Journals encourage students to make personal connections with the text, a valuable starting point for constructing their own understanding. As students become accustomed to and proficient with responding in a journal, they can be encouraged or guided to do more text analysis, employing higher-level thinking about the content.

Steps

1. Actively responding in a journal prompts thoughtful reactions to the selection and its relevance to students' lives or to life in general. As they make such connections while reading, students will come to a deeper understanding of the literature. As students are preparing to read a selection or a full-length book on their own, explain to them the reason for and importance of responding to literature. Ask students to give examples of things they might be thinking as they read their favorite genres. Have them be as specific and detailed as they can. Write students' ideas on the board.

2. Explain to students that in addition to the ideas they stated, there are many other things they might think about as they read. Pass out copies of the Response Journal Starters sheet. Review some of the stems on it. Model how you might apply some of them by reading aloud a portion of a selection the class is reading or has recently read. Encourage students to participate.

    If necessary, take time to go through the list of starters with the class to ensure that students have a general understanding of what they mean. You might mention at what points in a selection certain starters may be particularly appropriate.

3. As students are preparing to read a new selection or a full-length book, pass out copies of the Two-Column Response Journal sheet. Model how to use this sheet, applying some of the response starters. Tell students to record their quotations in the left column and their responses to the quotation in the right column, using the response starters. As they use a starter, they may check it off on the sheet. Encourage students to use as many of the starters as they can.

4. When students have finished reading and responding, ask for volunteers to share their quotations and responses or have students share in groups. Encourage disagreement and discussion. Exposure to one another's responses will expand students' views of the responding possibilities. Have students staple the Response Starters sheet to the front of their Two-Column Response sheets. Students may save their work in a folder or notebook. Sharing personal responses is not necessary; it may be valuable as students are learning this strategy, but thereafter the strategy may be better as a personal one.

You may want some students to expand their Two-Column Response Journal sheets into a dialogue journal that they share with a partner. Tell them to add a third column labeled My Partner's Response. Then, have them exchange papers with a partner and react to the partner's responses through comments or questions. Partners should discuss their new ideas and insights at the end of the activity.

5. Point out to students that their responses to any reading are not limited to the response starters. They may respond in other ways as well, depending on their own insights into or feelings about what they are reading. When reading a selection from *Prentice Hall Literature*, they may also respond to the questions in the right margins.

6. Assign or encourage students to use Response Journals when reading any literature on their own. The ongoing practice will heighten their attention to the literary texts they read. Students might like to set up a notebook as a Response Journal and use it exclusively for this purpose.

7. To make students accountable, you might collect and read their Response Journals and provide constructive feedback on them.

Source

Ollmann, H.E. (1992). "Two-Column Response to Literature." *Journal of Reading*, 35:58.

Response Journal Starters

- I wonder what will happen when . . .

- Does this mean that . . . ?

- I notice that . . ., which is interesting because . . .

- There is a lot of truth in this statement because . . .

- Life is like this when . . .

- This reminds me of . . .

- This sounds like another story, . . .

- I think what will happen next is . . .

- If I were this character, I would have . . .

- I bet the next thing this character will do is . . .

- I like the words . . . because . . .

- This description really made me appreciate how . . .

- The author is trying to make us see that . . .

- This is different from my time/culture because . . .

- This seems very realistic/unrealistic because . . .

- I do not like . . . because . . .

- If I were to rewrite this part, I would . . .

- At first I thought . . ., but now I think . . .

- Now I understand that . . .

Name _____ Class _____ Date _____

Two-Column Response Journal

Directions: Use this page for responses as you read. On the left side, copy quotations from the text. Choose sentences or passages that have particular meaning to you, that make you wonder about something, or anything else that strikes you and to which you wish to respond.

In the right column, next to each quotation, write your response. You may interpret the quotation, relate it to your own life, ask questions, evaluate it, comment on the writing style, or make any other kind of response.

Selection _____

Sentence or Passage from Selection	My Thoughts and Comments

Literature Circles

Description

Literature Circles are an excellent way to foster independent reading and responding within a collaborative group environment and an opportunity for students to go beyond their Response Journals. Students in Literature Circles not only collaborate to discover meaning; they develop responsibility and also have the pleasure of reading a good book and discussing it.

A Literature Circle is a temporary group formed to read and discuss books. The circle meets regularly, and each student takes on a specific role in the discussion. These discussions, based on students' own responses, involve a minimum of teacher intervention. Although Literature Circles have a structure and specified roles, they can be modified to accommodate a variety of circumstances and needs.

Steps

1. To introduce Literature Circles, tell students a little about the kinds of reading groups many adults belong to—the group chooses a book, and all the members read and discuss it.

2. To set up your Literature Circles, assign or allow students to choose appropriate titles from the Prentice Hall/Penguin Literature Library. Set up groups of four or five students to read and discuss one book. Interest students in the books by displaying the books in class and telling a little about each one. Allow students to examine the books, by looking at the front and back covers and flipping through the pages.

3. The roles of the participants in Literature Circles are important to the success of this strategy. You may assign roles for the duration of a Literature Circle, or you may have students rotate roles with each meeting. Four roles are essential, but other roles may be accommodated as well. The following roles are essential:
   Discussion Director: Creates open-ended questions to guide group discussion.
   Literary Luminary: Selects quotations or details from the text to bring to the attention of the group.
   Connector: Points out ways that the reading connects to themselves, the group, or the world.
   Illustrator: Represents key scenes or ideas from the reading in some kind of drawing.

   Literature Circles may also have participants in the following roles:
   Summarizer: Prepares a summary of the key points of each reading segment.
   Vocabulary Enricher: Clarifies meanings of important or unfamiliar words.

   It is important that students become familiar with the roles before they take them on. To help students organize and structure their responses, give each group three or four copies of Roles in Literature Circles. Students may use these sheets as guides and reminders for their roles and to make notes in preparation for the discussion. (They will probably need additional paper to record their ideas for their group discussions.) You might model and practice the roles with a selection the whole class reads together.

Some students may find the defined roles too limiting. Remind them that they are not required to focus only on these roles. Encourage them to think of other roles that group participants might play—for example, someone to get information on various places mentioned in a book.

4. Choose a reasonable time frame for students to finish reading their books. Students then meet once or twice a week, during class, to discuss the book in their Literature Circles. For example, you might allow three weeks for an average-length novel. For the first assignment, have students set up a reading schedule. They must determine the number of pages, with logical starting and stopping points, to read in preparation for each meeting.

5. As students read, encourage them to take notes or use sticky notes to mark passages that contain memorable ideas. They can also make notes using a Two-Column Response Journal.

6. When students meet in their groups, they should run their own discussions. (In the beginning, you will probably need to prompt them with questions or comments if their ideas flounder.) Tell them to refer to *all* the notes they have prepared when they talk about their books, not just the Roles in Literature Circles sheet.

7. When a group has finished a book, you might ask the members to tell the class about it. Encourage them to tell just enough to get other students interested in reading it. When all groups are finished reading, have students make new book choices and form new groups.

Source

Daniels, H. (2002). *Literature Circles: Voice and Choice in Book Clubs and Reading Groups*, 2nd ed. Portland, ME: Stenhouse.

Name _____ Class _____ Date _____

Roles in Literature Circles

Discussion Director: Ask Questions	For example: • How well can I identify with these characters and situations? • What seems likely to happen next? • What events seem likely? unlikely? YOUR IDEAS:
Literary Luminary: Look for the Best Parts	For example: • Identify a section, a piece of dialogue, or an event that really struck you; tell why. • Figure out how to get the group to appreciate this part. YOUR IDEAS:
Connector: Connect Ideas	For example: • Connect to things you have experienced at home, at school, or in your personal life. • Connect to what is going on in the world right now. YOUR IDEAS:
Illustrator: Put Ideas into Pictures	For example: • Draw a picture of an important event or character. • Draw a diagram that shows how you reacted to something in the book. YOUR IDEAS:

Save the Last Word for Me

Description

To become thoughtful, responsive readers, students need to be encouraged to think about more than finding answers to questions or commenting on characters or plot. Save the Last Word for Me is an excellent strategy for developing active and reflective readers by eliciting responses to specific quotations or passages from literature. The small group setting gives students an opportunity to interact meaningfully about a selection or a full-length work as they learn how to respond thoughtfully and completely and to justify their responses. In addition to encouraging those who may be reluctant to speak in front of the full class, the format also gives students time to rehearse their comments by writing them first.

Steps

1. This strategy works well with selections that are rich and potentially interesting to students. Prepare students to read by establishing background knowledge and clarifying vocabulary in your prereading activities. If working with a full-length book, you might apply this strategy to chapters or use it when students have completed the entire work.

2. Have students read the assigned work independently. Instruct them to note three to five statements or ideas that catch their attention as they read. These may be ideas with which they agree or disagree, that they find amusing, surprising, or intriguing, that reveal something about a character or an event in a story, or that are powerfully or eloquently stated. Provide students with sticky notes to mark these ideas.

3. After students have finished reading, give them copies of the Save the Last Word for Me response page. Tell students to go back and copy the statements that caught their attention onto this response sheet in the left column in the boxes above the dotted line. Then, have them paraphrase each statement they quoted—put it in their own words—in the boxes under the dotted line.

   If some students need more instruction or support on paraphrasing, provide a paraphrasing prompt, such as "I think this means _____ because _____."

4. After students have paraphrased each quotation, ask them to react to each. Students can begin by writing one sentence stating their reaction to it. Then students should write two or three sentences explaining or justifying the reaction. Modeling the technique for students at this point is important.

   For students who need more modeling of responding, you could read aloud several paragraphs from the story and note every time an idea strikes you. Model how to respond: agree, disagree, find interesting or surprising, share a personal experience, or relate to something else. Always explain or justify your reaction.

5. After students have written their responses, they gather in groups of three or four. The first student reads one of his or her quotations aloud along with the paraphrase, but not the reaction. The other group members respond to and discuss the quotation. When the other students have responded, the original student then reads his or her reaction, thus having the last word on the quotation. Then, the next person in the group reads his or her quotation and paraphrase, and the procedure continues as before until each person in the group has shared a statement and had the last word on it. You may then continue with another round of statements.

6. When students have finished, bring the class together to debrief. Did writing down ideas make students read more carefully and thoughtfully? Did their group members' responses make them think about their quotations in a different way? What ideas did they hear that were particularly interesting or surprising?

7. As an alternative to the Save the Last Word for Me Response Page, students may use index cards or paper folded in half, one card or sheet per statement.

Sources

Buehl, D. (2001). *Classroom Strategies for Interactive Learning.* Newark, DE: International Reading Association.
Vaughan, J., and Estes, T. (1986). *Reading and Reasoning Beyond the Primary Grades.* Boston: Allyn and Bacon.

Name _____ Class _____ Date _____

Save the Last Word for Me Response Page

My Quotations and Paraphrases	My Reactions

ReQuest (Reciprocal Questioning)

Description

ReQuest, an acronym for Reciprocal Questioning, is an instructional strategy designed by A. V. Manzo to help students develop an active, questioning approach as they read instructional materials. The ReQuest procedure promotes strategic learning by teaching students how to establish appropriate purposes for reading, and it enhances students' comprehension by teaching them to ask their own questions about what they are reading. When students ask themselves questions while reading, they are more likely to comprehend the text and to monitor their comprehension. The approach encourages students to read literature in-depth, noticing significant details and thinking beyond the surface.

It is important that you model effective questioning behaviors during the ReQuest procedure. Less experienced readers need to learn how to move beyond relatively simple text-based questions to more demanding interpretive or applied questions. As students become used to the strategy, they gradually assume more responsibility in the process.

Steps

1. Model the process by reading a brief section of the text aloud. Ask and answer your own questions about the text, progressing from factual recall to questions that stimulate interpretive or applied thinking.

2. After modeling this question-and-response pattern with a brief passage, ask students to read the next section of the text. With less proficient readers, consider reading the section aloud and having them read along silently. Have students take turns asking you questions about what they read, which you will then answer.

3. Ask students to read another segment. Ask them questions, which they answer.

4. Continue to alternate between student-generated questions and teacher-generated questions until the entire designated section has been read.

5. Assign the remaining portion for students to read silently, asking and answering their own questions. Then, lead a wrap-up discussion of the material.

6. Reinforce this questioning technique until students are comfortable applying it on their own. For students who may need more instruction and support, provide a manageable list of potential questions and question types. Many inexperienced younger readers are somewhat familiar with basic questions for narrative texts but need to go beyond the surface.

Sources

Manzo, A.V. (1969). "The ReQuest Procedure." *Journal of Reading*, 13:123–126.
Manzo, A.V., Manzo, U.C., and Estes, T.H. (2001). *Content Area Literacy: Interactive Teaching for Active Learning*, 3rd ed. Hoboken, NJ: John Wiley & Sons.

Question-Answer Relationships (QAR)

Description

Question-Answer Relationships (Raphael, 1982, 1986) is a strategy that helps students differentiate among various types of comprehension questions, enabling them to tackle questions more effectively.

The relationship between questions and the source of answers is not always obvious to students. Some questions are based solely on the text students are reading. These text-based questions may be text explicit ("right there") or text implicit ("think and search").

- **Right there** questions pick up exact words and phrases from the text. Students should be able to find the answers explicitly stated. These types of questions often begin with words like *Who is, Where is, When, What kind of,* and so on.

- **Think and search** questions are more challenging. Information is available in the text but requires integration of the text material. Students have to think about what they have read, search through a selection, and integrate information for an answer. These questions often include words such as *explain, summarize, compare, contrast,* and *what caused.*

Other types of questions require students to use their own knowledge and/or information from the text.

- **Author and you** questions ask students to synthesize what they already know with new information they have just learned. Students will not find ready-made answers in the text. Instead, they will have to put text information together with applicable prior knowledge.

- **On my own** questions test what students know from sources beyond the text. Students can answer these questions without having read the text by drawing on their own knowledge and experience.

Steps

1. Introduce students to the task demands of different types of questions. Explain the types of question-answer relationships and demonstrate them with examples from a selection the class is reading, progressing from factual recall to questions that test students' critical-thinking skills and background knowledge. Explain how and where to find the answers.

2. Once students have grasped the relationships, give them questions labeled by relationship and have them find the answers.

3. As students become competent, pose questions without labels or direct them to the questions in the text and instruct them to develop answers and decide which question-answer relationship applies.

4. Reinforce as necessary when students might be having difficulty answering questions in the text.

Sources

Raphael, T.E. Question-answering Strategies for Children. *The Reading Teacher*, 36:186–190.
Raphael, T.E. "Teaching Question-Answer Relationships Revisited," *The Reading Teacher*, 39:516–522.
Tierney, R.J. and Readence, J.E. (2000). *Reading Strategies and Practices: A Compendium.* Boston: Allyn and Bacon.

Reading Log

Description

A Reading Log with reader's comments and personal responses reflects accumulated reading accomplishments. Reading Logs are often required elements of school portfolios and mandated in state curriculums. Log pages should be kept in the classroom files.

Accurate Reading Logs are diagnostic tools for teachers, providing data of reading patterns and levels. Students can utilize Reading Logs as a tool for comparison, an outline for studying, or a method of activating prior knowledge.

Steps

1. Provide the students with several Reading Log pages. Students translate the number of pages into reading expectations.

2. Explain the type of reading that is to be recorded. It is useful to ask students to record reading in other subject areas as well.

3. Define *comments.* Comments should be a brief reaction to the work with reasons. To differentiate instruction, give a range of questions the students may use to form comments, such as the following scaffolded questions:

   - What did you like or dislike about the main character?

   - What did you learn from the main character?

   - Would you read this book again? Why or why not?

   - If you could talk to the author, what would you suggest be changed in the book? Why?

   - If you were a publisher, would you have published this book? Why or why not?

4. Designate 5 to 10 minutes a week to update Reading Logs. This should be on the same day at approximately the same time so that logging becomes part of the students' routine. Updating logs serves as a reminder to students of their reading accomplishments for the week and can be used as a summary activity.

   Check that the Reading Logs are returned to their designated classroom storage area at the end of each session.

5. Periodically write phrase comments on the Reading Logs so students are aware that you are checking their logs. Comments need not be lengthy or time consuming.

Reading Log

Directions: Use this log to keep a record of the books you read and your comments on those books.

Title	Author	Type of Literature	Date Finished	Comments

Interpretation Chart

Description

This close reading exercise is designed to give students practice in paraphrasing text and integrating the specific idea into the whole work. The Interpretation Chart asks students to choose a quotation that is important thematically, paraphrase the quotation to restate in their own words, and then determine why the quoted line is an important piece of the whole. Charts may be used as a basis for Literature Circle discussions, textual evidence for essays, or in large group discussion.

Steps

1. Choose a chapter or short selection to work with.

2. Preview the reading with students. Ask students to read the selection, noting important passages. Students may underline, use sticky notes, or write down the page number. They should not stop their reading to write down the entire quotation.

3. Ask students to return to the quotations they marked and choose two to copy onto the chart.

4. Model paraphrasing of one quotation. Demonstrate how to change sentence structure and wording.

5. Have students paraphrase one of the quotations.

6. Return to the model and discuss why this quotation is important to the whole work. (You may use a checklist of elements of the novel to help structure students' thinking.)

7. Ask students to write the "Why Is It Important" for their first quotation. Select two or three to read out loud as an informal check on understanding.

8. Students should fill in the chart for the second quotation individually.

9. Check that students are connecting the paraphrased quotation to the third column.

10. Ask students to complete the remainder of the chart.

Interpretation Chart

Directions: Use the following chart to help organize your thoughts on one or more aspects of a work of literature. In the first column, provide quotations from the work. In the second column, paraphrase each of the quotations. Finally, in the third column, discuss why the quoted line is important to the work.

Selection _____

What Does It Say?	What Does It Mean?	Why Is It Important?

Paired Discussion

Description

Paired Discussion encourages students to listen to another point of view and use that information to modify their own thoughts. The use of pairs encourages reluctant speakers to express their opinions. Paired Discussion also reinforces summary and paraphrasing skills and develops interpretation skills.

Preparing the Assignment

Choose a question based on a reading assignment that is appropriate to the middle thinking level of the class. The question should be presented to the students in writing so that they can reread. Write the question on the board, use an overhead, or dictate. Give the students thinking time; the length of time will depend on the depth and breadth of the question you ask.

Rules

- Set a time limit and stick to it.
- Explain that only one person may speak at a time and their partner should not interrupt them. Encourage students to note a question and return to it when their discussion partner is finished speaking.
- Monitor the discussions to see that students are on task.

Steps

1. Check that students have the required text on their desk. Then, give them the question.

2. Allow students 5–10 minutes to think about the question and return to the text to find examples.

3. Have students write their responses in the "My Response" column.

4. One person in the pair reads his or her response. The other person paraphrases the response and writes it down in the "My Partner's Response" column. Repeat this process with the second person in the pair.

5. Allow 5–10 minutes for students to ask each other questions regarding the responses.

6. Break down the third column into two thinking sections for the students. Ask students to individually fill in the "What I Think Now" portion of the third column. Instruct students to reread their statement of "What I Think Now."

7. Ask students to fill in the "and Why" section of the third column and then exchange papers with their partners to read.

8. Summarize the exercise by having volunteers read their sequence. Emphasize that listening to someone else's perspective can modify your own thinking.

Name _____ Class _____ Date _____

Paired Discussion

Directions: When working with a partner in a Paired Discussion, use the following chart to record your responses. In the first column, note your initial responses to the discussion question. Note your partner's responses in the second column. Finally, in the third column, note whether your responses changed as a result of your discussion and explain why or why not.

My Response	My Partner's Response	What I Think Now and Why

Think-Write-Pair-Share

Description

Think-Write-Pair-Share encourages students to verbally respond to open-ended questions and incorporates organizing, applying, and generating thinking and writing skills. This strategy emphasizes thinking time, which forces think-on-their-feet learners to evaluate their ideas and gives students who do not think on their feet adequate time to prepare; hence, it is a valuable tool in differentiated instruction. Think-Write-Pair-Share asks students to consider a teacher-posed question, organize answers, discuss responses with a partner, and develop a response to report to the class. The strategy assures that each student will have verbal discussion practice.

Steps

1. **Preparing the assignment**
   Time: Thinking time should start at three to five minutes depending on the material students have to review. Discussion time should be short, one to three minutes at first, with increased time as students become comfortable with the process.
   Topic: Clarify the topic and define the types of support that are acceptable to validate the topic. Check that the question cannot be answered by a yes or no. Clarify the thinking time stage.
   Roles: Assign partners to create productive matches. Define who is the first speaker. Define behavioral expectations.

2. **Pose a question to the entire class** The question should allow for responses on different thinking levels. Give students two to three minutes to write a paraphrase of the question. Randomly ask students to read their paraphrase as a check on question recognition.

3. **Think** Provide quiet, individual time for students to deal with the question. They may go back to the text, review notes, or organize their thoughts.

4. **Writing to prepare** (Optional) Ask students to write their responses in draft form. This gives the teacher a chance to provide additional clarification, modeling, or examples.

5. **Pair-Share** Remind students of time frames and cue them to begin discussion with their partners. During discussion, the students should take notes on similarities and differences. Listeners should encourage their partner to clarify, explain, and justify responses. Cue students when to switch listener/speaker roles.

6. **Share with the class** After rehearsing and elaborating their responses with a partner, students are invited to share in a whole-class discussion.

Source

Kagan, Spencer. (1992). Cooperative Learning. Kagan Cooperative Learning.

Name _____ Class _____ Date _____

Think-Write-Pair-Share

Directions: Use the following chart to help organize your thoughts on your teacher's question. Discuss your answers with your partner.

Paraphrase question: Restate the question in your own words.	
Information gathering: What do I need to gather to answer this question?	
Organizing: How do I put this information together so it forms an answer?	
Writing: What is my answer to the question? How do I support that answer?	
Pair Share: Listener List the points the speaker is making. Underline points that could be clearer.	
Pair Share: Speaker List points that need clarification.	
Response to share with class:	

Give One, Get One

Description

The typical question-and-answer protocols of many classroom discussions require spontaneous processing rather than active listening, conscientious reflection, and articulate responding. Give One, Get One is a productive alternative to the typical teacher-facilitated discussion format. This student-centered strategy allows students to share relevant background knowledge and experiences with partners before reporting new understandings during a unified class discussion. A multimodal strategy builds critical listening, speaking, reading, and writing skills. Students begin with quiet, independent reflection and writing time in response to a focused question or task. They then converse with classmates, one at a time. The goal of each interaction is to explain ideas and to obtain new ideas. After sharing ideas, students add one idea from the partner's list to their own. They then venture on to a new classmate. This procedure continues for a designated time. In the final stage, the teacher facilitates a highly structured, unified class debriefing. One student begins by sharing an idea learned from a peer. The student whose contribution has just been explained is next to report a new idea. Students must actively listen for their idea.

Steps

1. **Pose a thought-provoking question or concrete task** The question may be from any stage of a lesson, to activate prior knowledge, to make predictions and inferences, to assess comprehension, or to apply new understanding. The first few times you work with this strategy, select a question that you are confident all students will be able to answer.

2. **Preparing for participation** Give students five to eight minutes of quiet time to jot down responses. Specify the minimum number of responses you would like to see to push students to think beyond their initial response.

3. **Regrouping** Each student should draw a line after their final idea to differentiate this idea from those to be gathered from classmates. They should then put a check mark next to the two or three ideas he or she perceives as the strongest.

4. **Exchanging ideas** Students are given a set amount of time to share ideas with classmates. After each student finds a partner, the two classmates exchange papers and quietly read each other's ideas. Each student should comment on anything of particular interest on the other's list or ask for clarification. Each student then selects one idea from the other's list and adds it to his or her own list, noting the partner's name next to the idea.

5. **Debriefing** At the end of the Give One, Get One exchange period, the teacher facilitates a unified class debriefing of ideas. Record each idea along with the student's name on the board. This list can later be used as a springboard for practicing or teaching organizational strategies.

Name _____ Class _____ Date _____

Selection _____

Give One, Get One

Directions: Paraphrase the question posed by your teacher. Then, take a few minutes to record your responses to the question. After sharing ideas with classmates, record one idea from each partner's list on the chart. Make sure to note each partner's name next to his or her idea.

Paraphrase of question:

_____

_____

_____

My ideas:

1. _____

   _____

2. _____

   _____

3. _____

   _____

4. _____

   _____

5. _____

   _____

My Partners' Ideas	My Partners' Names
1.	
2.	
3.	
4.	
5.	

Discussion Guide

As you study literature, you will find that your discussions with other readers will help you develop interpretations of the works you read. Use the following tips to help you practice the good speaking and listening skills necessary for success in group discussions:

- **Communicate effectively** Effective communication requires thinking before speaking. Plan the points that you want to make and decide how you will express them. Organize these points in logical order and cite details from the work to support your ideas. Also, remember to speak clearly, pronouncing words slowly and carefully.

- **Make relevant contributions** Especially when responding to literature, avoid simply summarizing the plot. Instead, consider *what* you think might happen next, *why* events took place as they did, or *how* a writer provoked a response in you. Let your ideas inspire deeper thought or discussion about the literature that you are reading.

- **Consider other ideas and interpretations** One of the exciting parts of literature study is the varied responses that a work can generate in readers. Be open to the idea that many interpretations can be valid. To support your own ideas, point to the events, descriptions, characters, or other literary elements in the work that led to your interpretation. To consider someone else's ideas, decide whether details in the work support the interpretation he or she presents.

- **Ask questions** Get in the habit of asking questions. This can help you clarify your understanding of another reader's ideas. Questions can also be used to call attention to possible areas of confusion or debate or to errors in the speaker's points. When discussions become interactive, you can take your analysis and understanding of a work further.

As you meet with a discussion group, use a chart such as the following to analyze the discussion:

Work Being Discussed:	
Focus Questions:	
Your Response:	Another Student's Response:
Supporting Evidence:	Supporting Evidence:
One New Idea That You Considered About the Work During the Discussion:	

Writing Rubrics
Listening and Speaking Rubrics

Rubrics for Self-Assessment
Descriptive Essay

Evaluate your descriptive essay using one of the following rubrics:

Descriptive Essay—4-point rubric

	Audience and Purpose	Organization	Elaboration	Use of Language
Score 4	Creates a memorable main impression that is supported with the effective use of many sensory details	Is organized consistently, logically, and effectively	Contains rich sensory language that appeals to the five senses	Uses vivid and precise adjectives; contains no errors in grammar, punctuation, or spelling
Score 3	Creates a main impression through the use of details	Is organized consistently	Contains some rich sensory language	Uses some vivid and precise adjectives; contains few errors in grammar, punctuation, and spelling
Score 2	Contains details that distract from the main impression	Is organized but not consistently	Contains some rich sensory language, but it appeals to only one or two of the senses	Uses few vivid and precise adjectives; contains some errors in grammar, punctuation, and spelling
Score 1	Contains details that are unfocused and create no main impression	Is disorganized and confusing	Contains only flat language	Uses no vivid adjectives; contains many errors in grammar, punctuation, and spelling

Descriptive Essay—5-point rubric

Criteria	Rating Scale				
	Not Very				Very
Focus: How clear is the main impression?	1	2	3	4	5
Organization: How clear is your organization?	1	2	3	4	5
Support/Elaboration: How effectively do you use sensory details in your description?	1	2	3	4	5
Style: How vivid is the language used?	1	2	3	4	5
Conventions: How correct is your grammar, especially your use of possessive nouns?	1	2	3	4	5

Descriptive Essay—6-point rubric

	Audience and Purpose	Organization	Elaboration	Use of Language
Score 6	Creates a memorable main impression that is supported with the effective use of many sensory details	Well organized, with strong transitions helping to link words and ideas	Vivid, sensory details support main idea; the creative use of figurative language provides interesting comparisons	Varies sentence structures and makes good word choices; very few errors in spelling, grammar, or punctuation
Score 5	Creates a strong main impression that is supported with relevant sensory details	Clearly organized, although an occasional lapse may occur	Sensory details strongly support the main idea; figurative language beginning to make interesting comparisons	Some sentence variety and good word choices; some errors in spelling, grammar, or punctuation, but they do not interfere with reader understanding
Score 4	Creates a main impression that is supported by sensory details	Is consistently organized, although perhaps simplistically	Sensory details support main idea; figurative language used to create comparisons	Sentence structures and word choices may be appropriate but are occasionally awkward; errors in spelling, grammar, or punctuation may occur, but they do not interfere with reader understanding
Score 3	May create a main impression but does not adequately support it with sensory details	May have organization in some parts but lacks organization in other parts	Details in support of main idea are not consistently effective; attempts at figurative language not always successful or interesting	Inconsistent control of sentence structures and incorrect word choices; errors in spelling, grammar, or punctuation occasionally interfere with reader understanding
Score 2	Sensory details may be present but do not add up to a clear main impression	Very disorganized and not easy to follow	Limited use of sensory details in support of main idea; unsuccessful use of figurative language	Problematic sentence structures and frequent inaccuracies in word choices; errors in spelling, grammar, and punctuation hinder reader understanding
Score 1	Contains details that are unfocused or do not work in support of a clear main impression	Lacks organization and is confusing and difficult to follow; may be too brief to assess organization	No sensory details used in support of main idea; no figurative language	Little or no control over sentences and incorrect word choices may cause confusion; many errors in spelling, grammar, and punctuation severely hinder reader understanding

Rubrics for Self-Assessment
Autobiographical Narrative

Evaluate your autobiographical narrative using one of the following rubrics.

Autobiographical Narrative—4-point rubric

	Audience and Purpose	Organization	Elaboration	Use of Language
Score 4	Contains an engaging introduction; successfully entertains or presents a theme	Creates an interesting, clear narrative; told from a consistent point of view	Provides insight into characters; develops plot; contains dialogue	Uses word choices and tone to reveal the story's theme; contains noerrors in grammar, punctuation, or spelling
Score 3	Contains a somewhat engaging introduction; entertains or presents a theme	Presents a clear sequence of events; told from a specific point of view	Contains details and dialogue that develop characters and plot	Uses interesting and fresh word choices; contains few errors in grammar, punctuation, and spelling
Score 2	Contains an introduction; attempts to entertain or to present a theme	Presents a mostly clear sequence of events; contains inconsistent points of view	Contains details that develop plot; contains some dialogue	Uses some clichés and trite expressions; contains some errors in grammar, punctuation, and spelling
Score 1	Begins abruptly or confusingly; leaves purpose unclear	Presents events without logical order; lacks a consistent point of view	Contains few or no details to develop characters or plot	Uses uninspired word choices; has many errors in grammar, punctuation, and spelling

Autobiographical Narrative—5-point rubric

Criteria	Rating Scale				
	Not Very				Very
Focus: How clearly does the narrative present the problem or conflict?	1	2	3	4	5
Organization: How clearly is the sequence of events presented?	1	2	3	4	5
Support/Elaboration: How effective are details in describing people, places, and events?	1	2	3	4	5
Style: How well does the language grab the reader's interest?	1	2	3	4	5
Conventions: How correct is your grammar, especially your use of pronouns and antecedents?	1	2	3	4	5

Autobiographical Narrative—6-point rubric

	Audience and Purpose	Organization	Elaboration	Use of Language
Score 6	Clearly addresses the writing prompt; a main idea is clearly presented	Well organized, with strong transitions helping to link words and ideas	The story is effectively developed with elaborated support and specific details; may contain dialogue	Varies sentence structures and makes good word choices; very few errors in spelling, grammar, or punctuation
Score 5	Clearly addresses the writing prompt by telling an engaging story	Clearly organized, although an occasional lapse may occur	The story is developed with support and details; may contain dialogue	Some sentence variety and good word choices; some errors in spelling, grammar, or punctuation, but they do not interfere with reader understanding
Score 4	Addresses the writing prompt by telling a complete story	Is consistently organized, although perhaps simplistically	Contains details and/or dialogue that help to develop story	Sentence structures and word choices are appropriate; errors in spelling, grammar, or punctuation may occur, but they do not interfere with reader understanding
Score 3	Attempts to tell a story but does not do so completely; introduction or theme may be present but not developed	May have organization in some parts but lacks organization in other parts	Contains details and/or dialogue that help to develop the story but may not consistently do so	Inconsistent control of sentence structures and incorrect word choices; errors in spelling, grammar, or punctuation occasionally interfere with reader understanding
Score 2	Minimal attempt to tell a story; limited development of theme	Very disorganized and not easy to follow	Limited details in support of the story	Problematic sentence structures and frequent inaccuracies in word choices; errors in spelling, grammar, and punctuation hinder reader understanding
Score 1	Little or no attempt is made to address the prompt; response is unfocused or undeveloped	Lacks organization and is confusing and difficult to follow; may be too brief to assess organization	Few or no details given to develop the story	Little or no control over sentences and incorrect word choices may cause confusion; many errors in spelling, grammar, and punctuation severely hinder reader understanding

Rubrics for Self-Assessment
Response to Literature

Evaluate your response to literature using one of the following rubrics:

Response to Literature—4-point rubric

	Audience and Purpose	Organization	Elaboration	Use of Language
Score 4	Presents sufficient background on the work(s); presents the writer's reactions forcefully	Presents points in a logical order, smoothly connecting them to the overall focus	Supports reactions and evaluations with elaborated reasons and well-chosen examples	Shows overall clarity and fluency; uses precise, evaluative words; makes few mechanical errors
Score 3	Presents background on the work(s); presents the writer's reactions clearly	Presents points in a logical order and connects many to the overall focus	Supports reactions and evaluations with specific reasons and examples	Shows good sentence variety; uses some precise evaluative terms; makes some mechanical errors
Score 2	Presents some background on the work(s); presents the writer's reactions at points	Organizes points poorly in places; connects some points to an overall focus	Supports some reactions and evaluations with reasons and examples	Uses awkward or overly simple sentence structures and vague evaluative terms; makes many mechanical errors
Score 1	Presents little or no background on the work(s); presents few of the writer's reactions	Presents information in a scattered and disorganized manner	Offers little support for reactions and evaluations	Presents incomplete thoughts; makes mechanical errors that create confusion

Response to Literature—5-point rubric

Criteria	Rating Scale				
	Not Very				Very
Focus: How clearly have you focused on an interesting aspect of the story?	1	2	3	4	5
Organization: How well are ideas, patterns, or images organized?	1	2	3	4	5
Support/Elaboration: How convincing are the supporting details for each main idea?	1	2	3	4	5
Style: How well have you stated your feelings or judgments?	1	2	3	4	5
Conventions: How correct is your grammar, especially your use of irregular verbs?	1	2	3	4	5

Response to Literature—6-point rubric

	Audience and Purpose	Organization	Elaboration	Use of Language
Score 6	Clearly focuses on one aspect of the text, with sufficient summary information provided	Well organized, with strong transitions helping to link words and ideas	Develops any assertions with elaborated support and details from the text; provides the writer's reactions to the text	Varies sentence structures and makes good word choices; very few errors in spelling, grammar, or punctuation
Score 5	Focuses on one aspect of the text, with summary information provided	Clearly organized, although an occasional lapse may occur	Develops any assertions with support from the text; provides the writer's reactions to the text	Some sentence variety and good word choices; some errors in spelling, grammar, or punctuation, but they do not interfere with reader understanding
Score 4	Mainly focuses on one aspect of the text, with general summary information given	Is consistently organized, although perhaps simplistically	Adequate support for the main idea is provided, as well as some of the writer's reaction to the text	Sentence structures and word choices are appropriate; errors in spelling, grammar, or punctuation may occur, but they do not interfere with reader understanding
Score 3	Some summary information is given, but the focus is not clear	May have organization in some parts but lacks organization in other parts	Support for the main idea is not fully developed; writer's reactions may not be emphasized	Inconsistent control of sentence structures and incorrect word choices; errors in spelling, grammar, or punctuation occasionally interfere with reader understanding
Score 2	An unsuccessful attempt is made to discuss the text; either topic is unclear or support is limited	Very disorganized and not easy to follow	Support is repetitive or undeveloped, with little discussion of the writer's reactions	Problematic sentence structures and frequent inaccuracies in word choices; errors in spelling, grammar, and punctuation hinder reader understanding
Score 1	Not fully engaged in the task; either the text is not discussed or no attempt is made to support ideas	Lacks organization and is confusing and difficult to follow; may be too brief to assess organization	Lacks support, summary information, or writer's reactions	Little or no control over sentences and incorrect word choices may cause confusion; many errors in spelling, grammar, and punctuation severely hinder reader understanding

Rubrics for Self-Assessment
Short Story

Evaluate your short story using one of the following rubrics:

Short Story—4-point rubric

	Audience and Purpose	Organization	Elaboration	Use of Language
Score 4	Contains an engaging introduction; successfully entertains or presents a theme	Creates an interesting and clear narrative; told from a consistent point of view	Provides insight into characters; develops plot; contains dialogue	Uses word choices and tone to reveal story's theme; contains no errors in grammar, punctuation, or spelling
Score 3	Contains a somewhat engaging introduction; entertains or presents a theme	Presents a clear sequence of events; told from a specific point of view	Contains details and dialogue that develop characters and plot	Uses interesting and fresh word choices; contains few errors in grammar, punctuation, and spelling
Score 2	Contains an introduction; attempts to entertain or to present a theme	Presents a mostly clear sequence of events; contains inconsistent points of view	Contains details that develop plot; contains some dialogue	Uses some clichés and trite expressions; contains some errors in grammar, punctuation, and spelling
Score 1	Begins abruptly or confusingly; leaves purpose unclear	Presents events without a logical order; lacks a consistent point of view	Contains few or no details to develop characters or plot	Uses uninspired word choices; has many errors in grammar, punctuation, and spelling

Short Story—5-point rubric

Criteria	Rating Scale				
	Not Very				Very
Focus: How well drawn are the characters?	1	2	3	4	5
Organization: How clearly organized is the story's plot?	1	2	3	4	5
Support/Elaboration: How well do the details and language establish the setting?	1	2	3	4	5
Style: How consistently have you used point of view?	1	2	3	4	5
Conventions: How correct is your grammar, especially your use of verb tenses?	1	2	3	4	5

General Resources

Short Story—6-point rubric

	Audience and Purpose	Organization	Elaboration	Use of Language
Score 6	Successfully narrates the events of the story; captures the interest of the audience	Creates an interesting and clear narrative; told from a consistent point of view	Provides insight into characters; contains dialogue that develops characters and furthers the plot	Uses word choices and tone to reveal story's theme; contains minor errors in grammar, punctuation, and spelling
Score 5	Narrates the events of the story; contains details that appeal to an audience	Displays a clear sequence of events; told from a specific point of view	Contains details and language that establish setting and characters	Uses interesting word choices; contains few errors in grammar, punctuation, and spelling
Score 4	Includes some details that contribute to its purpose or that appeal to an audience	Includes some inconsistencies of organization; told from a point of view	Develops characters with details but has some vague words; includes good use of dialogue	Uses unimaginative word choices; contains some errors in grammar, punctuation, and spelling
Score 3	Contains few details that contribute to its purpose or that appeal to an audience	Displays lapses in organization; contains inconsistent points of view	Provides some details to develop characters; contains some dialogue	Uses clichés and unoriginal expressions; has several errors in grammar, punctuation, and spelling
Score 2	Presents weak narrative and purpose; provides little appeal to an audience	Presents a weak or unclear connection between ideas or events	Includes little dialogue; does not sufficiently develop characters	Uses awkward or overly simple sentence structures; contains many errors in grammar, punctuation, and spelling
Score 1	Leaves purpose unclear; is not written for a specific audience	Presents events in no logical order; lacks a consistent point of view	Contains few or no details to develop characters; does not provide dialogue	Includes incomplete thoughts; creates confusion through errors in grammar, punctuation, and spelling

Rubrics for Self-Assessment
How-to Essay

Evaluate your how-to essay using one of the following rubrics:

How-to Essay—4-point rubric

	Audience and Purpose	Organization	Elaboration	Use of Language
Score 4	Clearly focuses on procedures leading to a well-defined end	Gives instructions in a logical order; subdivides complex actions into steps	Provides appropriate amount of detail; gives needed explanations	Shows overall clarity and fluency; uses transitions effectively; contains few mechanical errors
Score 3	Focuses on procedures leading to a well-defined end	Gives instructions in logical order; subdivides some complex actions into steps	Provides appropriate amount of detail; gives some explanations	Shows some sentence variety; uses some transitions; includes few mechanical errors
Score 2	Includes procedures related to an end but presents some vaguely	Generally gives instructions in a logical order	Provides some detail; gives few explanations	Uses awkward or overly simple sentence structures; contains many mechanical errors
Score 1	Includes only vague descriptions of procedures and results	Gives instructions in a scattered and disorganized manner	Provides few details; gives few or no explanations	Contains incomplete thoughts and confusing mechanical errors

How-to Essay—5-point rubric

Criteria	Rating Scale				
	Not Very				Very
Focus: How well have you focused your topic?	1	2	3	4	5
Organization: How organized is the sequence of steps and the list of materials?	1	2	3	4	5
Support/Elaboration: How helpful are illustrations or diagrams?	1	2	3	4	5
Style: How well do you use transitions to make the steps clear?	1	2	3	4	5
Conventions: How correct is your grammar, especially your use of modifiers?	1	2	3	4	5

How-to Essay—6-point rubric

	Audience and Purpose	Organization	Elaboration	Use of Language
Score 6	Clearly focuses on the topic being explained	Well organized, with strong transitions helping to link words and ideas	Provides all specific, relevant steps needed to complete the task; fully explains any unfamiliar terms to the audience	Varies sentence structures and makes good word choices; very few errors in spelling, grammar, or punctuation
Score 5	Clearly focuses on the topic being explained	Clearly organized, although an occasional lapse may occur	Provides specific steps needed to complete the task; explains any unfamiliar terms to the audience	Some sentence variety and good word choices; some errors in spelling, grammar, or punctuation, but they do not interfere with reader understanding
Score 4	Focuses on the topic being explained	Is consistently organized, although perhaps simplistically	Provides steps needed to complete the task	Sentence structures and word choices are appropriate; errors in spelling, grammar, or punctuation may occur, but they do not interfere with reader understanding
Score 3	Although a topic may be identified, the directions given to complete the task are not fully explained	May have organization in some parts but lacks organization in other parts	Some explanation is given, but steps may be missing or terms could be used that could confuse the audience	Inconsistent control of sentence structures and incorrect word choices; errors in spelling, grammar, or punctuation occasionally interfere with reader understanding
Score 2	The topic may be unclear; only a minimal attempt is made at explaining how to complete a task	Very disorganized and not easy to follow	Steps needed to complete task are not all provided or are repetitive and confusing	Problematic sentence structures and frequent inaccuracies in word choices; errors in spelling, grammar, and punctuation hinder reader understanding
Score 1	Not fully engaged in the task; a task to be completed may not be identified	Lacks organization and is confusing and difficult to follow; may be too brief to assess organization	Lacks support or no attempt is made to explain the procedure	Little or no control over sentences and incorrect word choices may cause confusion; many errors in spelling, grammar, and punctuation severely hinder reader understanding

Rubrics for Self-Assessment
Persuasive Essay

Evaluate your persuasive essay using one of the following rubrics:

Persuasive Essay—4-point rubric

	Audience and Purpose	Organization	Elaboration	Use of Language
Score 4	Provides arguments, illustrations, and words that forcefully appeal to the audience and effectively serve the persuasive purpose	Uses a clear and consistent organizational strategy	Provides specific, well-elaborated support for the writer's position	Uses transitions to connect ideas smoothly; shows few mechanical errors
Score 3	Provides arguments, illustrations, and words that appeal to the audience and serve the persuasive purpose	Uses a clear organizational strategy with occasional inconsistencies	Provides some elaborated support for the writer's position	Uses some transitions; shows few mechanical errors
Score 2	Provides some support that appeals to the audience and serves the persuasive purpose	Uses an inconsistent organizational strategy	Provides some support but with little elaboration	Uses few transitions; shows some mechanical errors
Score 1	Shows little attention to the audience or the persuasive purpose	Shows a lack of organizational strategy; writing is confusing	Lacks support	Shows little connection between ideas; shows many mechanical errors

Persuasive Essay—5-point rubric

Criteria	Rating Scale				
	Not Very				Very
Focus: How clearly is your position stated?	1	2	3	4	5
Organization: How organized is the introduction, body, and conclusion?	1	2	3	4	5
Support/Elaboration: How well are facts, statistics, examples, and reasons presented?	1	2	3	4	5
Style: How powerful are the images and language used?	1	2	3	4	5
Conventions: How correct is your grammar, especially your use of coordinating conjunctions?	1	2	3	4	5

Persuasive Essay—6-point rubric

	Audience and Purpose	Organization	Elaboration	Use of Language
Score 6	Clearly states the author's position and effectively persuades the reader of the validity of the author's argument	Well organized, with strong transitions helping to link words and ideas	Develops its arguments with specific, well-elaborated support	Varies sentence structures and makes good word choices; very few errors in spelling, grammar, or punctuation
Score 5	Clearly states the author's position and persuades the reader	Clearly organized, although an occasional lapse may occur	Develops its arguments with specific support	Some sentence variety and good word choices; some errors in spelling, grammar, or punctuation, but they do not interfere with reader understanding
Score 4	States a position and adequately attempts to persuade the reader	Is consistently organized, although perhaps simplistically	Provides some elaborated support of the author's position	Sentence structures and word choices are appropriate; errors in spelling, grammar, or punctuation may occur, but they do not interfere with reader understanding
Score 3	Although a position may be stated, either it is unclear or undeveloped	May have organization in some parts but lacks organization in other parts	The support of the position may be brief, repetitive, or irrelevant	Inconsistent control of sentence structures and incorrect word choices; errors in spelling, grammar, or punctuation occasionally interfere with reader understanding
Score 2	Either a position is not clearly given or little attempt is made at persuasion	Very disorganized and not easy to follow	The support of the position is not well developed	Problematic sentence structures and frequent inaccuracies in word choices; errors in spelling, grammar, and punctuation hinder reader understanding
Score 1	Little effort is made to persuade because there is no position taken or because no support is given	Lacks organization and is confusing and difficult to follow; may be too brief to assess organization	Lacks support	Little or no control over sentences and incorrect word choices may cause confusion; many errors in spelling, grammar, and punctuation severely hinder reader understanding

Rubrics for Self-Assessment
Writing for Assessment Essay

Evaluate your writing for assessment essay using one of the following rubrics:

Writing for Assessment Essay—4-point rubric

	Audience and Purpose	Organization	Elaboration	Use of Language
Score 4	Uses word choices and supporting details appropriate to the specified audience; clearly addresses writing prompt	Presents a clear and consistent organizational strategy	Adequately supports the thesis; elaborates each idea; links all details to the thesis	Uses excellent sentence variety and vocabulary; includes very few mechanical errors
Score 3	Mostly uses word choices and supporting details appropriate to the specified audience; adequately addresses prompt	Presents a clear organizational strategy with few inconsistencies	Supports the thesis; elaborates most ideas; links most information to the thesis	Uses adequate sentence variety and vocabulary; includes few mechanical errors
Score 2	Uses some inappropriate word choices and details; addresses writing prompt	Presents an inconsistent organizational strategy	Partially supports the thesis; does not elaborate some ideas	Uses repetitive sentence structures and vocabulary; includes some mechanical errors
Score 1	Uses inappropriate word choices and details; does not address writing prompt	Shows a lack of organizational strategy	Provides no thesis; does not elaborate ideas	Demonstrates poor use of language; includes many mechanical errors

Writing for Assessment Essay—5-point rubric

Criteria	Rating Scale				
	Not Very				Very
Focus: How clearly is the thesis statement or main idea stated?	1	2	3	4	5
Organization: How well does your organization suit your answer to the writing prompt?	1	2	3	4	5
Support/Elaboration: How well did you use details, facts, and reasons for support?	1	2	3	4	5
Style: How well did you use language that directly answers the question?	1	2	3	4	5
Conventions: How correct is your grammar, especially your use of punctuation?	1	2	3	4	5

Writing for Assessment Essay—6-point rubric

	Audience and Purpose	Organization	Elaboration	Use of Language
Score 6	Clearly addresses the writing prompt; a main idea is clearly presented	Well organized, with strong transitions helping to link words and ideas	The thesis is effectively developed with elaborated support and specific details and ideas	Varies sentence structures and makes good word choices; very few errors in spelling, grammar, or punctuation
Score 5	Clearly addresses the writing prompt; a main idea is presented	Clearly organized, although an occasional lapse may occur	The thesis is developed with elaborated support and details	Some sentence variety and good word choices; some errors in spelling, grammar, or punctuation, but they do not interfere with reader understanding
Score 4	Addresses the writing prompt; a main idea is presented	Is consistently organized, although perhaps simplistically	The thesis is adequately supported	Sentence structures and word choices are appropriate; errors in spelling, grammar, or punctuation may occur, but they do not interfere with reader understanding
Score 3	Although the prompt may be addressed, the main idea may not be clear	May have organization in some parts but lacks organization in other parts	The support given for the thesis may be unclear or undeveloped	Inconsistent control of sentence structures and incorrect word choices; errors in spelling, grammar, or punctuation occasionally interfere with reader understanding
Score 2	An attempt is made to address the prompt; however, either the topic is unclear or the support is limited	Very disorganized and not easy to follow	Limited support or support that does not substantiate a clear main idea	Problematic sentence structures and frequent inaccuracies in word choices; errors in spelling, grammar, and punctuation hinder reader understanding
Score 1	Little or no attempt is made to address the prompt; the response is unfocused or undeveloped	Lacks organization and is confusing and difficult to follow; may be too brief to assess organization	Lacks elaboration of ideas	Little or no control over sentences and incorrect word choices may cause confusion; many errors in spelling, grammar, and punctuation severely hinder reader understanding

Rubrics for Self-Assessment
Comparison-and-Contrast Essay

Evaluate your comparison-and-contrast essay using one of the following rubrics:

Comparison-and-Contrast Essay—4-point rubric

	Audience and Purpose	Organization	Elaboration	Use of Language
Score 4	Clearly attracts audience interest in the comparison-and-contrast analysis	Clearly presents information in a consistent organization best suited to the topic	Elaborates ideas with facts, details, or examples; uses all information for comparison and contrast	Demonstrates excellent sentence and vocabulary variety; includes very few mechanical errors
Score 3	Adequately attracts audience interest in the comparison-and-contrast analysis	Presents information using an organization suited to the topic	Elaborates most ideas with facts, details, or examples; uses most information for comparison and contrast	Demonstrates adequate sentence and vocabulary variety; includes few mechanical errors
Score 2	Provides a reason for the comparison-and-contrast analysis	Chooses an organization not suited to comparison and contrast	Does not elaborate all ideas; does not use enough details for comparison and contrast	Demonstrates repetitive use of sentence structures and vocabulary; includes many mechanical errors
Score 1	Does not provide a reason for a comparison-and-contrast analysis	Shows a lack of organizational strategy	Does not provide facts or examples to support a comparison and contrast	Demonstrates poor use of language; generates confusion; includes many mechanical errors

Comparison-and-Contrast Essay—5-point rubric

Criteria	Rating Scale				
	Not Very				Very
Focus: How clearly does the topic state how two or more subjects are alike and different?	1	2	3	4	5
Organization: How effective are your points of comparison organized?	1	2	3	4	5
Support/Elaboration: How well do you use facts, descriptions, and examples to describe similarities and differences?	1	2	3	4	5
Style: How effective is your language in grabbing the reader's interest?	1	2	3	4	5
Conventions: How correct is your grammar, especially your use of compound complements?	1	2	3	4	5

Comparison-and-Contrast Essay—6-point rubric

	Audience and Purpose	Organization	Elaboration	Use of Language
Score 6	Clearly presents a topic to be compared and contrasted and targets audience	Well organized, with strong transitions helping to link words and ideas	Effectively elaborates similarities and differences with details and examples as support	Varies sentence structures and makes good word choices; very few errors in spelling, grammar, or punctuation
Score 5	Provides a topic to be compared and contrasted and targets audience	Clearly organized, although an occasional lapse may occur	Elaborates similarities and differences with details and examples as support	Some sentence variety and good word choices; some errors in spelling, grammar, or punctuation, but they do not interfere with reader understanding
Score 4	Provides a topic to be compared and contrasted	Is consistently organized, although perhaps simplistically	Adequately addresses similarities and differences	Sentence structures and word choices are appropriate; errors in spelling, grammar, or punctuation may occur, but they do not interfere with reader understanding
Score 3	May attempt to compare and contrast two things but does not do so fully or clearly	May have organization in some parts but lacks organization in other parts	Does not consistently address similarities and differences; may emphasize some but neglect others	Inconsistent control of sentence structures and incorrect word choices; errors in spelling, grammar, or punctuation occasionally interfere with reader understanding
Score 2	Only a minimal attempt at comparing and contrasting two things; either topic is unclear or support is limited	Very disorganized and not easy to follow	Similarities and differences are not present or not well explained; support is minimal	Problematic sentence structures and frequent inaccuracies in word choices; errors in spelling, grammar, and punctuation hinder reader understanding
Score 1	Does not compare and contrast	Lacks organization and is confusing and difficult to follow; may be too brief to assess organization	Lacks support or elaboration	Little or no control over sentences and incorrect word choices may cause confusion; many errors in spelling, grammar, and punctuation severely hinder reader understanding

Rubrics for Self-Assessment
Letter

Evaluate your letter using one of the following rubrics:

Letter—4-point rubric

	Audience and Purpose	Organization	Elaboration	Use of Language
Score 4	Formally and clearly provides purposeful information; addresses the intended audience appropriately	Follows a standard format for business writing; uses a uniform typeface and spacing; effectively organizes information	Clearly states and supports the reasons for writing; highlights central ideas or images	Uses formal language that addresses the nature of the relationship with the recipients; introduces few, if any, mechanical errors
Score 3	Formally provides purposeful information; addresses the intended audience appropriately	Follows a standard format for business writing; uses a uniform typeface and spacing; logically organizes information	States and supports the reasons for writing; lists central ideas or images	Uses formal language that acknowledges the nature of the relationship with the recipients; introduces a few mechanical errors
Score 2	Formally provides information; does not clearly address the intended audience	Follows some formatting for business writing; logically organizes most information	States the reasons for writing, but needs more support for them; vaguely indicates central ideas or images	Uses formal language that unsuccessfully acknowledges the nature of the relationship with the recipients; introduces some mechanical errors
Score 1	Uses informal language; does not address the intended audience appropriately	Uses an inappropriate format for business writing; inconsistently or randomly presents information	Fails to state the reasons for writing; there are no central ideas or images	Uses language that does not acknowledge the nature of the relationship with the recipients; introduces many mechanical errors

Letter—5-point rubric

Criteria	Rating Scale				
	Not Very				**Very**
Focus: How clearly do you state your reaction to the author's work?	1	2	3	4	5
Organization: How well do you organize your letter using standard business format?	1	2	3	4	5
Support/Elaboration: How well do you use examples from the author's work to support your ideas?	1	2	3	4	5
Style: How formal and polite is the language?	1	2	3	4	5
Conventions: How correct is your grammar, especially your use of participial phrases?	1	2	3	4	5

Letter—6-point rubric

	Audience and Purpose	Organization	Elaboration	Use of Language
Score 6	Formally and clearly provides purposeful information; addresses the intended audience appropriately	Follows a standard format for business writing; uses a uniform typeface and spacing; effectively organizes information	Clearly states and supports the reasons for writing; highlights central ideas or images	Uses formal language that appropriately addresses the nature of the relationship with the recipients; introduces few, if any, grammatical and mechanical errors
Score 5	Formally provides purposeful information; addresses the intended audience appropriately	Follows a standard format for business writing; uses a uniform typeface and spacing; logically organizes information	States and supports the reasons for writing; lists central ideas or images	Uses formal language that acknowledges the nature of the relationship with the recipients; introduces a few grammatical and mechanical errors
Score 4	Formally provides information; sometimes does not clearly address the intended audience appropriately	Follows a standard format for business writing; logically organizes most information	States the reasons for writing but needs more support for them; indicates central ideas or images	Uses formal language that somewhat acknowledges the nature of the relationship with the recipients; introduces some grammatical and mechanical errors
Score 3	Formally provides information; does not clearly address the intended audience appropriately	Uses an appropriate format for business writing; organizes some information	States the reasons for writing but lacks support for them; central ideas or images are unclear	Uses formal language that does not acknowledge the nature of the relationship with the recipients; introduces some grammatical and mechanical errors
Score 2	Uses informal language; does not clearly address the intended audience appropriately	Uses an appropriate format for business writing; information often presented inconsistently or randomly	The reasons for writing are unclear and lack support; central ideas or images are limited	Uses language that does not acknowledge the nature of the relationship with the recipients; introduces numerous grammatical and mechanical errors
Score 1	Uses informal language; does not address the audience appropriately	Does not use an appropriate format; most information presented inconsistently or randomly	Fails to state the reasons for writing; there are no central ideas or images	Uses language that does not acknowledge the nature of the relationship with the recipients; introduces many grammatical and mechanical errors

Rubrics for Self-Assessment
Cause-and-Effect Essay

Evaluate your cause-and-effect essay using one of the following rubrics:

Cause-and-Effect Essay—4-point rubric

	Audience and Purpose	Organization	Elaboration	Use of Language
Score 4	Consistently targets an audience through word choices and details; clearly identifies the purpose in the thesis statement	Presents a clear and consistent organizational strategy to show cause and effect	Successfully links causes with effects; fully elaborates connections among ideas	Chooses clear transitions to convey ideas; presents very few mechanical errors
Score 3	Targets an audience through most word choices and details; identifies the purpose in the thesis statement	Presents a clear organizational strategy with occasional inconsistencies; shows cause and effect	Links causes with effects; elaborates connections among most ideas	Chooses transitions to convey ideas; presents few mechanical errors
Score 2	Misses a target audience by including a wide range of word choices and details; presents no clear purpose	Presents an inconsistent organizational strategy; creates an illogical presentation of causes and effects	Links some causes with some effects; elaborates connections among most ideas	Misses some opportunities for transitions to convey ideas; presents many mechanical errors
Score 1	Addresses no specific audience or purpose	Demonstrates a lack of organizational strategy; creates a confusing presentation	Develops and elaborates no links between causes and effects	Demonstrates poor use of language; presents many mechanical errors

Cause-and-Effect Essay—5-point rubric

Criteria	Rating Scale				
	Not Very				Very
Focus: How clearly is your thesis on cause and effect stated?	1	2	3	4	5
Organization: How effective is your organization?	1	2	3	4	5
Support/Elaboration: How convincing are the facts and details used for support?	1	2	3	4	5
Style: How well are transitions used to connect ideas?	1	2	3	4	5
Conventions: How correct is your grammar, especially your use of prepositional phrases?	1	2	3	4	5

General Resources

Cause-and-Effect Essay—6-point rubric

	Audience and Purpose	Organization	Elaboration	Use of Language
Score 6	Clearly identifies a cause-and-effect situation and effectively targets audience	Well organized, with strong transitions helping to link words and ideas	Effectively links causes with effects through relevant and elaborated support and details	Varies sentence structures and makes good word choices; very few errors in spelling, grammar, or punctuation
Score 5	Clearly identifies a cause-and-effect situation and targets audiences	Clearly organized, although an occasional lapse may occur	Links causes with effects through relevant support and details	Some sentence variety and good word choices; some errors in spelling, grammar, or punctuation, but they do not interfere with reader understanding
Score 4	Identifies a cause-and-effect situation and adequately addresses audience	Is consistently organized, although perhaps simplistically	Links causes with effects with some support	Sentence structures and word choices are appropriate; errors in spelling, grammar, or punctuation may occur, but they do not interfere with reader understanding
Score 3	A cause-and-effect situation may be identified, but it is not clear; target audience may not be addressed	May have organization in some parts but lacks organization in other parts	Although some support linking cause and effect may be present, it is not fully or consistently developed	Inconsistent control of sentence structure and incorrect word choices; errors in spelling, grammar, or punctuation occasionally interfere with reader understanding
Score 2	Only a minimal attempt at linking a cause and effect; either topic is unclear or support is limited	Very disorganized and not easy to follow	Support is very unclear or very undeveloped	Problematic sentence structure and frequent inaccuracies in word choice; errors in spelling, grammar, and punctuation hinder reader understanding
Score 1	Not fully engaged in the task; a cause and effect may not be identified	Lacks organization and is confusing and difficult to follow; may be too brief to assess organization	Lacks supports or no attempt is made to support the connection between cause and effect	Little or no control over sentences and incorrect word choices may cause confusion; many errors in spelling, grammar, and punctuation severely hinder reader understanding

Rubrics for Self-Assessment
Multimedia Report

Evaluate your multimedia report using one of the following rubrics:

Multimedia Report—4-point rubric

	Audience and Purpose	Organization	Elaboration	Use of Language
Score 4	Clearly and effectively presents a main topic appropriate to the intended audience	Uses appropriate word processing, audio, and visual formats to organize and present information	Includes a clear and consistent list of sources; uses visual and audio components to elaborate on and enhance written material	Presents facts and details to precisely address the topic; effectively uses language to integrate different types of media
Score 3	Clearly presents a main topic appropriate to the intended audience	Uses mostly appropriate word processing, audio, and visual formats to organize and present information	Includes a consistent list of sources; uses visual and audio components to elaborate on written material	Presents facts and details to adequately address the topic; uses language to integrate different types of media
Score 2	Presents a main topic that is somewhat inappropriate to the intended audience	Uses somewhat inappropriate word processing, audio, and visual formats to organize and present information	Includes a somewhat inconsistent list of sources; uses visual and audio components with a vague connection to written material	Presents facts and details to somewhat address the topic; attempts to use language to integrate different types of media
Score 1	Presents a vague main topic that is inappropriate to the intended audience	Fails to use appropriate word processing, audio, or visual formats to organize and present information	Includes an inconsistent list of sources; uses visual and audio components with little, if any, connection to written material	Presents facts and details but addresses the topic inadequately; fails to use language to integrate different types of media

Multimedia Report—5-point rubric

Criteria	Rating Scale Not Very				Very
Focus: How clearly do you state your main idea?	1	2	3	4	5
Organization: How effectively do you use formatting to enhance your presentation?	1	2	3	4	5
Support/Elaboration: How effectively do you use media elements, such as visuals and sound?	1	2	3	4	5
Style: How smooth are your transitions between elements?	1	2	3	4	5
Conventions: How correct is your grammar, especially your revision of sentence fragments?	1	2	3	4	5

Multimedia Report—6-point rubric

	Audience and Purpose	Organization	Elaboration	Use of Language
Score 6	Clearly and effectively identifies and introduces a main topic appropriate for the target audience	Uses a variety of appropriate word processing, audio, and visual formats to organize and present information; employs skillful transitions to link ideas and images in an effective order	Includes a clear and consistent list of sources; uses well-chosen visual and audio components to elaborate on and enhance written material	Presents well-chosen facts and details to precisely address the topic; effectively uses language to integrate different types of media smoothly
Score 5	Clearly identifies and introduces a main topic appropriate to the intended audience	Uses appropriate word processing, audio, and visual formats to organize and present information; employs transitions to link ideas and images	Includes a consistent list of sources; uses visual and audio components to elaborate on written material	Presents facts and details to adequately address the topic; uses language to integrate different types of media
Score 4	Presents a main topic appropriate to the intended audience	Uses mostly appropriate formats to organize and present information; connections between ideas and images are somewhat simplistic	Includes a somewhat consistent list of sources; uses visual and audio components that connect to written material	Uses facts and details that address the topic for the most part; uses language that attempts to integrate different types of media
Score 3	Presents a main topic that is somewhat appropriate to the intended audience	Uses somewhat inappropriate formats to organize and present information; connections between ideas and images are occasionally unclear	Includes a somewhat inconsistent list of sources; uses visual and audio components with a vague connection to written material	Uses facts and details that address the topic somewhat; attempts to use language to integrate different types of media
Score 2	Presents a main topic that is somewhat inappropriate to the intended audience	Includes inappropriate word processing, audio, and visual formats to present information; contains little organizational structure	Includes a very brief and inconsistent list of sources; uses visual or audio components with little or no connection to written material	Includes facts and details that are distracting and unrelated to the topic; uses language that fails to integrate different types of media
Score 1	Presents a vague main topic that is inappropriate for the intended audience	Fails to use appropriate word processing, audio, or visual formats to present information; fails to use a method of organization	Fails to include a list of sources; visual and audio components have no connection to written material	Presents some facts and details but addresses the topic inadequately; fails to use language to integrate different types of media

Rubrics for Self-Assessment
Research Report

Evaluate your research report using one of the following rubrics:

Research Report—4-point rubric

	Audience and Purpose	Organization	Elaboration	Use of Language
Score 4	Focuses on a clearly stated thesis, starting from a well-framed question; gives complete citations	Presents information in a logical order and emphasizes details of central importance	Draws clear conclusions from information gathered from multiple sources	Shows overall clarity and fluency; contains few mechanical errors
Score 3	Focuses on a clearly stated thesis; gives citations	Presents information in a logical order	Draws conclusions from information gathered from multiple sources	Shows good sentence variety; contains some errors in spelling, punctuation, or usage
Score 2	Focuses mainly on the chosen topic; gives some citations	Presents information logically, but organization is poor in places	Explains and interprets some information	Uses awkward or overly simple sentence structures; contains many mechanical errors
Score 1	Presents information without a clear focus; few or no citations	Presents information in a scattered and disorganized manner	Presents information with little or no interpretation or synthesis	Contains incomplete thoughts and mechanical errors that make the writing confusing

Research Report—5-point rubric

Criteria	Not Very	Rating Scale			Very
Focus: How clearly is your topic stated?	1	2	3	4	5
Organization: How clear is the method of organization?	1	2	3	4	5
Support/Elaboration: How well do facts, details, examples, and explanations support the main ideas?	1	2	3	4	5
Style: How smooth are your transitions?	1	2	3	4	5
Conventions: According to an accepted format, how complete and accurate are your citations?	1	2	3	4	5

Research Report—6-point rubric

	Audience and Purpose	Organization	Elaboration	Use of Language
Score 6	Focuses on a clearly stated topic, starting from a well-framed question	Well organized, with strong transitions helping to link words and ideas	Provides information, facts, and details in support of topic; emphasizes details of greatest importance	Varies sentence structures and makes good word choices; very few errors in spelling, grammar, or punctuation
Score 5	Focuses on a clearly stated topic	Clearly organized, although an occasional lapse may occur	Provides information, facts, and details in support of topic; some emphasis on more important details	Some sentence variety and good word choices; some errors in spelling, grammar, or punctuation, but they do not interfere with reader understanding
Score 4	Focuses on topic	Is consistently organized, although perhaps simplistically	Provides information, facts, and details in support of topic	Sentence structures and word choices are appropriate; errors in spelling, grammar, or punctuation may occur, but they do not interfere with reader understanding
Score 3	Topic may be clear, but focus does not remain consistently on it	May have organization in some parts but lacks organization in other parts	Some information, facts, and details about topic but also includes extraneous, ill-chosen, or unnecessary details	Inconsistent control of sentence structures and incorrect word choices; errors in spelling, grammar, or punctuation occasionally interfere with reader understanding
Score 2	Little emphasis on a single, clear topic	Very disorganized and not easy to follow	Information or details in support of topic are undeveloped or unclear	Problematic sentence structures and frequent inaccuracies in word choices; errors in spelling, grammar, and punctuation hinder reader understanding
Score 1	No focus on a single, clear topic	Lacks organization and is confusing and difficult to follow; may be too brief to assess organization	No clear support of a main topic in the form of information, facts, or details	Little or no control over sentences and incorrect word choices may cause confusion; many errors in spelling, grammar, and punctuation severely hinder reader understanding

Rubrics for Self-Assessment
Problem-Solution Essay

Evaluate your problem-solution essay using one of the following rubrics:

Problem-Solution Essay—4-point rubric

	Audience and Purpose	Organization	Elaboration	Use of Language
Score 4	Clearly states and explains the problem; uses strong and convincing language that is appropriate to the specified audience	Distinctly differentiates between the problem and its possible solutions; organizes the steps or parts of the solution in a clear and logical manner	Clearly explains several possible solutions; strongly supports possible solutions with detailed reasons and examples	Effectively uses transitions to connect ideas; consistently avoids run-on sentences
Score 3	States and describes the problem; uses convincing language that is appropriate to the specified audience	Differentiates between the problem and its possible solutions; organizes the steps or parts of the solution in a logical manner	Explains one or more possible solutions; includes some reason or examples to support possible solutions	Uses many transitions to connect ideas; includes one or two run-on sentences
Score 2	States and briefly describes the problem; uses unconvincing language that is mostly appropriate to the specified audience	Blurs the distinction between the problem and its possible solutions; organizes the steps or parts of the solution in a somewhat logical manner	Explains one possible solution; includes one or two reasons and examples for support	Uses some transitions to connect ideas; includes several run-on sentences
Score 1	Fails to state the problem and explains it vaguely; uses unconvincing language that is somewhat inappropriate to the specified audience	Fails to distinguish between the problem and its possible solutions; does not use an apparent organizational strategy	Mentions one possible solution but fails to explain it; includes a few reasons but no examples for support	Uses few, if any, transitions to connect ideas; uses mostly run-on sentences

Problem-Solution Essay—5-point rubric

Criteria	Rating Scale Not Very				Very
Focus: How clearly is the problem stated and explained?	1	2	3	4	5
Organization: How organized are the steps or parts of the solution?	1	2	3	4	5
Support/Elaboration: How strong and convincing is the support?	1	2	3	4	5
Style: How effectively are transitions used to connect ideas?	1	2	3	4	5
Conventions: How consistently does the writer avoid run-on sentences?	1	2	3	4	5

Problem-Solution Essay—6-point rubric

	Audience and Purpose	Organization	Elaboration	Use of Language
Score 6	Clearly states and explains the problem; proposes solution; uses convincing language to address target audience	Clearly differentiates between the problem and its possible solutions; organizes the steps or parts of the solution in a clear and logical manner	Clearly explains several possible solutions; strongly supports possible solutions with detailed reasons and examples	Varies sentence structures and makes good word choices; effectively uses transitions to connect ideas; very few errors in spelling, grammar, or punctuation
Score 5	Sufficiently states and describes the problem and proposes solution; uses language that is appropriate to target audience	Differentiates between the problem and possible solutions; organizes steps in a logical manner	Explains possible solutions; includes reasons and examples to support possible solutions	Includes some sentence variety and good word choices; uses transitions to connect ideas; contains some errors in spelling, grammar, or punctuation
Score 4	Describes problem and proposes solution; generally addresses target audience	Is organized, although coherence could be improved with more efficient use of transitions to link words and ideas	Provides one or more possible solutions; offers some details to support the possible solutions	Sentence structures and word choices are appropriate; uses some transitions to connect ideas
Score 3	States and briefly describes the problem; briefly refers to a solution; addresses audience in unconvincing language	Blurs the distinction between the problem and its possible solutions; organizes the steps of the solution in a somewhat logical manner	Briefly explains one possible solution; support for the solution is spotty and is lacking sufficient detail	Inconsistent control of sentence structures and incorrect word choices; errors in spelling, grammar, or punctuation occasionally interfere with reader understanding
Score 2	Some attempt may be made to identify a problem and solution, but either the topic is unclear or the support is limited	Weak organization; confusing and difficult to follow	Mentions one possible solution but fails to explain it; includes a few reasons but no examples for support	Problematic sentence structures and frequent inaccuracies in word choices; uses few transitions to connect ideas; errors in spelling, grammar, and punctuation hinder reader understanding
Score 1	Fails to state the problem and explains it vaguely; uses unconvincing language that is inappropriate to the audience	Fails to distinguish between the problem and its possible solutions; does not use any apparent organizational strategy	Fails to identify or explain reasonable solution; lacks support and has no details or examples	Little or no control over sentences and incorrect word choices may cause confusion; many errors in spelling, grammar, and punctuation severely hinder reader understanding

Rubrics for Self-Assessment
Summary

Evaluate your summary using one of the following rubrics:

Summary—4-point rubric

	Audience and Purpose	Organization	Elaboration	Use of Language
Score 4	Clearly and effectively projects the deeper meaning of the work being summarized; reflects the writer's own understanding	Clearly states the main idea; includes the most significant details	Includes only the essential details and explains their significance and relevance to the main idea	Effectively connects ideas with transitions; uses language that is brief and concise
Score 3	Projects a grasp of the deeper meaning of the work being summarized; reflects the writer's own understanding	States the main idea; includes important details, but some may not be significant	Includes mostly essential details and somewhat explains their significance and relevance to the main idea	Connect ideas with transitions; uses language that is mostly brief and concise
Score 2	Projects a sense of the deeper meaning of the work being summarized; indicates the writer's own understanding	Indicates the main idea somewhat vaguely; includes important details, but some may not be significant	Includes some inessential details and vaguely explains their significance and relevance to the main idea	Uses some transitions to connect ideas; uses language that is not as brief and concise as prescribed by a summary format
Score 1	Projects little awareness of the deeper meaning of the work being summarized; shows a lack of the writer's own understanding	Fails to include the main idea; includes some details, but most are insignificant	Includes random details that may or may not be significant and fails to explain their relevance to the main idea	Uses few, if any, transitions to connect ideas; uses language that is not brief and concise

Summary—5-point rubric

Criteria	Rating Scale				
	Not Very				**Very**
Focus: How well does the summary reflect the deeper meaning of the work?	1	2	3	4	5
Organization: How clear is the statement of the main idea?	1	2	3	4	5
Support/Elaboration: How significant are the details?	1	2	3	4	5
Style: How brief and precise is the writing?	1	2	3	4	5
Conventions: How effective are the transitions?	1	2	3	4	5

Summary—6-point rubric

	Audience and Purpose	Organization	Elaboration	Use of Language
Score 6	Clearly and effectively expresses the deeper meaning of the work being summarized; precisely reflects the writer's own understanding	Clearly and powerfully states the main idea; includes the most significant details	Includes the most essential details; clearly explains their significance and relevance to the main idea	Smoothly and effectively connects ideas with transitions; uses compelling language that is brief and concise
Score 5	Expresses the deeper meaning of the work being summarized; accurately reflects the writer's own understanding	Clearly states the main idea; includes significant details	Includes essential details; explains their significance and relevance to the main idea	Effectively connects ideas with transitions; uses language that is brief and concise
Score 4	Expresses a grasp of the deeper meaning of the work being summarized; adequately reflects the writer's own understanding	States the main idea; includes important details, but some may not be significant	Includes mostly essential details; somewhat explains their significance and relevance to the main idea	Connects ideas with transitions; uses language that is mostly brief and concise
Score 3	Expresses a limited sense of the deeper meaning of the work being summarized; shows a lack of the writer's own understanding	States the main idea somewhat vaguely; includes important details, but some may not be significant	Includes some inessential details; vaguely explains their significance and relevance to the main idea	Uses some transitions to connect ideas; uses language that is somewhat brief and concise
Score 2	Expresses little awareness of the deeper meaning of the work being summarized; shows a lack of the writer's own understanding	States the main idea vaguely; includes some details, but many are insignificant	Includes random details that may or may not be significant; fails to explain their relevance to the main idea	Uses few transitions to connect ideas; uses language that is not brief and concise
Score 1	Fails to express the deeper meaning of the work being summarized; shows a lack of the writer's own understanding	Fails to state the main idea; includes random details, most or all of which are insignificant	Fails to include significant details; fails to explain their relevance to the main idea	Fails to use transitions to connect ideas; uses language that is not brief and concise

Rubrics for Self-Assessment
Poem (Rhyming)

Evaluate your poem using one of the following rubrics:

Poem (Rhyming)—4-point rubric

	Rhythm and Sound	Structure and Form	Figurative Language and Imagery	Effect on Reader
Score 4	Carries meaning and experience through rhythm and sound patterns; sound devices fit function	Form is appropriate to the subject; form and structure emphasize certain words and suggest meanings; pattern emphasizes words important to meaning	Uses vivid imagery that carries the poem's subject; effectively uses figurative language and conveys thoughts and emotion	Carries a powerful connection of thought, experience, and emotion
Score 3	Rhythm and sound patterns occasionally support meaning; patterns somewhat support function	Form is appropriate to the subject; form partially emphasizes words and meanings; an attempt at patterning is evident	Uses some imagery to carry the poem's subject; figurative language occasionally describes thought and emotion	Carries a sense of thought, experience, and emotion
Score 2	Lacks either rhythm or sound patterns; rhythm and sound infrequently support meaning or function	Form should be more appropriate to the subject; an attempt at patterning is limited	Uses unclear imagery and figurative language to describe experience or emotions	Briefly describes a sense of experience or emotion
Score 1	Lacks sound patterns and rhythm; sounds are random and do not support meaning or function	Fails to use apparent form and pattern	Imagery and figurative language are not present	Fails to relate experience or emotion

Poem (Rhyming)—5-point rubric

Criteria	Rating Scale				
	Not Very				Very
Rhythm and Sound: How clearly do your rhythm and sound patterns carry the meaning?	1	2	3	4	5
Structure and Form: How appropriate is your organization?	1	2	3	4	5
Figurative Language and Imagery: How effective is your use of figurative language and sensory details?	1	2	3	4	5
Effect on Reader: How well do you express the experience and emotions?	1	2	3	4	5

Poem (Rhyming)—6-point rubric

	Rhythm and Sound	Structure and Form	Figurative Language and Imagery	Effect on Reader
Score 6	Carries meaning and experience through rhythm and sound patterns; sound devices fit function	Form is appropriate to the subject; form and structure emphasize certain words and suggest meanings; pattern emphasizes words important to meaning	Uses vivid imagery that carries the poem's subject; effectively uses figurative language and conveys thoughts and emotion	Carries a powerful connection of thought, experience, and emotion
Score 5	Rhythm and sound patterns evident and generally support meaning; most sound devices fit function	Form fits function; form and structure occasionally emphasize certain words and suggest meanings; pattern is evident	Uses imagery to carry the poem's subject; uses figurative language to describe thought and emotion	Carries a connection of thought, experience, and emotion
Score 4	Rhythm and sound patterns occasionally support meaning; patterns somewhat support function	Form is appropriate to the subject; form partially emphasizes words and meanings; an attempt at patterning is evident	Uses some imagery to carry the poem's subject; figurative language occasionally describes thought and emotion	Carries a sense of thought, experience, and emotion
Score 3	Rhythm and sound patterns are present but may not support meaning; sound devices inconsistently fit function	An attempt at form is evident; attempts to provide pattern	Uses unclear imagery and figurative language to describe experience or emotions	Briefly describes a sense of experience or emotion
Score 2	Lacks either rhythm or sound patterns; rhythm and sound infrequently support meaning or function	Form should be more appropriate to the subject; an attempt at patterning is limited	Contains insufficient imagery and figurative language to describe experience, emotions, or thought	Attempts to describe experience or emotion
Score 1	Lacks sound patterns and rhythm; sounds are random and do not support meaning or function	Fails to use apparent form and pattern	Imagery and figurative language are not present	Fails to relate experience or emotion

Rubrics for Self-Assessment
Critique

Evaluate your critique using one of the following rubrics:

Critique—4-point rubric

	Audience and Purpose	Organization	Elaboration	Use of Language
Score 4	Uses arguments, illustrations, and word choices that clearly appeal to a specific audience; clearly projects knowledge of the subject and point of view	Presents points in a logical order; uses a clear and consistent organization	Effectively supports and elaborates all key points of the critique	Effectively uses transitions to connect ideas; shows very few mechanical errors
Score 3	Uses arguments, illustrations, and word choices that usually appeal to a specific audience; projects knowledge of the subject and point of view	Presents points in order; shows some inconsistency in overall organization	Supports the main points of the critique with some elaboration	Uses some transitions to connect ideas; shows some mechanical errors
Score 2	Provides some support that occasionally appeals to a specific audience; shows some knowledge of the subject and point of view	Uses an inconsistent organization	Provides some support of the critique but with little elaboration	Uses few transitions to connect ideas; shows many mechanical errors
Score 1	Addresses no specific audience or purpose; shows little or no knowledge of the subject or point of view	Lacks organization and is confusing and difficult to follow	Provides little, if any, relevant or reasonable support	Uses few, if any, transitions to connect ideas; contains many mechanical errors that hinder reader understanding

Critique—5-point rubric

Criteria	Rating Scale				
	Not Very				Very
Focus: How clear are your position and purpose?	1	2	3	4	5
Organization: How consistent and logical is your organization?	1	2	3	4	5
Support/Elaboration: How well do you elaborate support for ideas?	1	2	3	4	5
Style: How clear and fluent are your sentences?	1	2	3	4	5
Conventions: How accurate is your use of spelling, grammar, and punctuation?	1	2	3	4	5

Critique—6-point rubric

	Audience and Purpose	Organization	Elaboration	Use of Language
Score 6	Uses arguments, illustrations, and word choices that clearly appeal to a specific audience; clearly projects knowledge of the subject and point of view	Presents points in logical order; uses a clear and consistent organization	Effectively supports and elaborates all key points of the critique	Effectively uses transitions to connect ideas; shows very few mechanical errors
Score 5	Uses arguments, illustrations, and word choices that adequately appeal to a specific audience; projects knowledge of the subject and point of view	Presents points in a logical order; uses clear organization with few inconsistencies	Supports and elaborates most key points of the critique	Uses transitions to connect ideas; shows few mechanical errors
Score 4	Uses arguments, illustrations, and word choices that usually appeal to a specific audience; projects knowledge of the subject and point of view	Presents points in order; shows some inconsistency in overall organization	Supports the main points of the critique with some elaboration	Uses some transitions to connect ideas; shows some mechanical errors
Score 3	Provides some support that occasionally appeals to a specific audience; shows some knowledge of the subject and point of view	Organizes some points; uses an inconsistent organization	Provides some support of the critique, but with little elaboration	Uses some transitions to connect ideas; contains many mechanical errors
Score 2	Provides little support that appeals to a specific audience; shows limited knowledge of the subject and point of view	Uses an inconsistent organization	Provides little support of the critique; does not elaborate	Uses few transitions to connect ideas; shows many mechanical errors
Score 1	Addresses no specific audience or purpose; shows little or no knowledge of the subject or point of view	Lacks organization and is confusing and difficult to follow	Provides little, if any, relevant or reasonable support	Uses few, if any, transitions to connect ideas; contains many mechanical errors that hinder reader understanding

Rubrics for Self-Assessment
Biography

Evaluate your biography using one of the following rubrics:

Biography—4-point rubric

	Audience and Purpose	Organization	Elaboration	Use of Language
Score 4	Contains an engaging introduction; a main idea is clearly presented	Well organized, with strong transitions helping to link words and ideas	The story is effectively developed with elaborated support and specific details; provides insight into characters	Varies sentence structures and makes good word choices; very few errors in spelling, grammar, or punctuation
Score 3	Contains a somewhat engaging introduction; addresses the main idea	May have organization in some parts but lacks organization in other parts	The story is developed with support and details; contains details and/or dialogue that help to develop characters	Some sentence variety and good word choices; several errors in spelling, grammar, or punctuation
Score 2	Attempts to tell a story but does not do so completely; limited development of theme	Disorganized and not easy to follow	Contains limited details in support of the story	Inconsistent control of sentence structures and inaccuracies in word choices; errors in spelling, grammar, and punctuation hinder reader understanding
Score 1	Little or no attempt is made to address the prompt; response is unfocused or undeveloped	Lacks organization and is difficult to follow; may be too brief to assess organization	Few or no details are given to develop story	Little or no control over sentences and incorrect word choices may cause confusion; many errors in spelling, grammar, and punctuation severely hinder reader understanding

Biography—5-point rubric

Criteria	Not Very	Rating Scale			Very
Focus: How well does the narrative present a strong introduction and theme?	1	2	3	4	5
Organization: How logical and consistent is your organization?	1	2	3	4	5
Support/Elaboration: How vivid are details and dialogue?	1	2	3	4	5
Style: How well do your transitions help to link words and ideas?	1	2	3	4	5
Conventions: How correct is your spelling, grammar, and punctuation?	1	2	3	4	5

Biography—6-point rubric

	Audience and Purpose	Organization	Elaboration	Use of Language
Score 6	Contains an engaging introduction; a main idea is clearly presented	Well organized, with strong transitions helping to link words and ideas	The story is effectively developed with elaborated support and specific details; provides insight into characters	Varies sentence structures and makes good word choices; very few errors in spelling, grammar, or punctuation
Score 5	Contains a somewhat engaging introduction; addresses the main idea	Clearly organized, although an occasional lapse may occur	The story is developed with support and details; contains details and dialogue that develop characters	Some sentence variety and good word choices; occasional errors in spelling, grammar, or punctuation, but they do not interfere with reader understanding
Score 4	Contains an interesting introduction; tells a complete story	Is consistently organized, although perhaps simplistically	Contains details and/or dialogue that help to develop story and characters	Sentence structures and word choices are appropriate; several errors in spelling, grammar, or punctuation may occur
Score 3	Attempts to tell a story but does not do so completely; introduction or theme may be present but not developed	May have organization in some parts but lacks organization in other parts	Contains details and/or dialogue that help to develop story but may not consistently do so	Inconsistent control of sentence structures and incorrect word choices; errors in spelling, grammar, or punctuation occasionally interfere with reader understanding
Score 2	Minimal attempt to tell a story; limited development of theme	Disorganized and not easy to follow	Contains limited details in support of the story	Problematic sentence structures and frequent inaccuracies in word choices; errors in spelling, grammar, and punctuation hinder reader understanding
Score 1	Little or no attempt is made to address the prompt; response is unfocused or undeveloped	Lacks organization and is difficult to follow; may be too brief to assess organization	Few or no details are given to develop story	Little or no control over sentences and incorrect word choices may cause confusion; many errors in spelling, grammar, and punctuation severely hinder reader understanding

Rubrics for Self-Assessment
Reader Response Journal

Evaluate your reader response journal using one of the following rubrics:

Reader Response Journal—4-point rubric

	Audience and Purpose	Organization	Elaboration	Use of Language
Score 4	The author's writing is discussed in great detail with specific examples; reflections are discussed with much depth and detail	Uses a clear and consistent organization	Provides specific, well-elaborated support of details and well-chosen examples	Shows overall clarity and fluency; makes very few mechanical errors
Score 3	Reflects on the author's writing; some key ideas are identified and explained with details and examples	Shows some inconsistency in overall organization	Provides some elaborated support of details and examples	Shows good sentence variety; makes some mechanical errors
Score 2	Reaction or reflection is lacking or not related to the text with examples	Presents an inconsistent organization	Provides some support, but with little elaboration	Contains little sentence variety; makes many mechanical errors
Score 1	No personal response or reflection is made	Demonstrates a lack of organization	Offers no support or elaboration	Demonstrates poor use of language; makes many mechanical errors that hinder reader understanding

Reader Response Journal—5-point rubric

Criteria	Not Very	Rating Scale			Very
Focus: How clear is your purpose?	1	2	3	4	5
Organization: How consistent is your organization?	1	2	3	4	5
Support/Elaboration: How well do you elaborate your support?	1	2	3	4	5
Style: How clear and fluent are your sentences?	1	2	3	4	5
Conventions: How accurate is your use of spelling, grammar, and punctuation?	1	2	3	4	5

Reader Response Journal—6-point rubric

	Audience and Purpose	Organization	Elaboration	Use of Language
Score 6	The author's writing is discussed in great detail with specific examples; reflections are discussed with much depth and detail	Uses a clear and consistent organization	Provides specific, well-elaborated support of details and well-chosen examples	Shows overall clarity and fluency; makes very few mechanical errors
Score 5	The author's writing is discussed clearly and is supported with evidence from the work	Uses a clear organization with few inconsistencies	Provides support and elaboration of specific details and examples	Shows good sentence variety; makes few mechanical errors
Score 4	Reflects on the author's writing; some key ideas are identified and explained with details and examples	Shows some inconsistency in overall organization	Provides some elaborated support of details and examples	Shows adequate sentence variety; makes some mechanical errors
Score 3	An opinion is expressed; some reflections are made with adequate support	May have organization in some parts, but lacks organization in other parts	Provides some support but with little elaboration	Shows some sentence variety; makes many mechanical errors
Score 2	Reaction or reflection is lacking or not related to the text with examples	Presents an inconsistent organization	Provides little support; does not elaborate	Contains little sentence variety; makes many mechanical errors
Score 1	No personal response or reflection is made	Demonstrates a lack of organization	Offers no support or elaboration	Demonstrates poor use of language; makes many mechanical errors that hinder reader understanding

Rubrics for Self-Assessment
Generic (Holistic) Writing:

Evaluate your writing assignment using one of the following rubrics:

Generic (Holistic) Writing—4-point rubric

	Audience and Purpose	Organization	Elaboration	Use of Language
Score 4	Displays strong focus on the task; consistently targets an audience through word choices and supporting details	Presents a clear and consistent organizational strategy	Fully develops the main idea; support is specific and substantial	Shows overall clarity and fluency; varies sentence structures; contains very few mechanical errors
Score 3	Identifies purpose; targets an audience through most word choices and details	Includes some inconsistencies of organization	Provides some support for ideas, but development may be uneven	Some sentence variety and good word choices; shows some mechanical errors
Score 2	The writing is related to the task but generally lacks focus	Demonstrates an inconsistent organization	Provides some support, but with little elaboration	Uses overly simple sentence structures; presents many mechanical errors
Score 1	Addresses no specific audience or purpose	Shows a lack of organizational strategy	Lacks support; does not elaborate ideas	Demonstrates poor use of language; contains many mechanical errors that hinder reader understanding

Generic (Holistic) Writing—5-point rubric

Criteria	Rating Scale				
	Not Very				Very
Focus: How clear is your purpose?	1	2	3	4	5
Organization: How consistent is your organization?	1	2	3	4	5
Support/Elaboration: How well do you elaborate support for ideas?	1	2	3	4	5
Style: How clear and fluent are your sentences?	1	2	3	4	5
Conventions: How accurate is your use of spelling, grammar, and punctuation?	1	2	3	4	5

Generic (Holistic) Writing—6-point rubric

	Audience and Purpose	Organization	Elaboration	Use of Language
Score 6	Displays strong focus on the task; consistently targets an audience through word choices and supporting details	Presents a clear and consistent organizational strategy	Fully develops main idea; support is specific and substantial	Shows overall clarity and fluency; varies sentence structures; contains very few mechanical errors
Score 5	Clearly focuses on the task; uses appropriate word choices and details	Presents a clear and consistent organizational strategy with few inconsistencies	Elaborates key ideas with relevant details	Uses sentence variety and good word choices; contains few mechanical errors
Score 4	Identifies purpose; targets an audience through most word choices and details	Includes some inconsistencies of organization	Supports main idea, but development may be uneven	Some sentence variety and good word choices; shows some mechanical errors
Score 3	Provides some support that appeals to the audience	Presents lapses or flaws in organization	Provides some support; does not elaborate all ideas	Uses simple sentence structures and incorrect word choices; shows some mechanical errors
Score 2	The writing is related to the task, but generally lacks focus	Demonstrates an inconsistent organization	Offers little support for ideas	Uses awkward or overly simple sentence structures; contains many mechanical errors
Score 1	Addresses no specific audience or purpose	Shows a lack of organizational strategy	Lacks support; does not elaborate ideas	Demonstrates poor use of language; contains many mechanical errors that hinder reader understanding

Rubric for Evaluating a Persuasive Presentation

Use the following rubric to assess evaluating persuasive presentations.

Rating System

+ = excellent   ✓ = average   — = weak

Content

Evaluates reliability and accuracy of information _____

Considers sources of information _____

Distinguishes between fact and opinion _____

Distinguishes between entertainment, persuasion, and factual information _____

Delivery

Recognizes persuasive techniques _____

Recognizes visual, auditory, and special effects _____

Recognizes the persuasive intent of the overall presentation _____

Ascertains the basic message of the overall presentation _____

Evaluation Summary

Persuasive techniques do not unduly influence evaluation _____

Sound reasoning is used to make a judgment about the message _____

A conclusion regarding the reliability of the message is reached _____

An appropriate evaluation of the message is made _____

Rubric for Analyzing Media Messages

Use the following rubric to assess analyzing media messages.

Rating System

+ = excellent	✓ = average	— = weak

Content
Analyzes images _____
Analyzes text _____
Analyzes sound _____
Listens for strong evidence _____
Distinguishes between entertainment, persuasion, and factual information _____

Delivery
Recognizes persuasive techniques _____
Recognizes visual, auditory, and special effects _____
Analyzes effects _____
Identifies the techniques used to achieve media effects _____
Recognizes the intent of the message _____

Evaluation Summary
Persuasive techniques do not unduly influence evaluation _____
Effects and the techniques used to achieve them are considered _____
Sound reasoning is used to make a judgment about the message _____
A conclusion regarding the message is reached _____
An appropriate evaluation of the message is made _____

Rubric for Evaluating Advertisements

Use the following rubric to assess evaluating advertisements.

Rating System

+ = excellent   ✓ = average   — = weak

Content

Evaluates content _____

Challenges the claims and the logic _____

Considers sources of information _____

Distinguishes between facts, effects, and persuasive techniques _____

Delivery

Evaluates delivery _____

Recognizes persuasive techniques _____

Analyzes entertainment effects _____

Analyzes emotional effects _____

Recognizes the persuasive intent of the advertisement _____

Evaluation Summary

Persuasive techniques do not unduly influence evaluation _____

Sound reasoning is used to make a judgment about the advertisement _____

A conclusion regarding the reliability of the advertisement is reached _____

An appropriate evaluation of the advertisement is made _____

Rubric for Evaluating a Media Presentation

Use the following rubric to assess evaluations of media presentations.

Content

Analyzes the effects of images, text, and sound _____

Identifies techniques used to achieve effects _____

Evaluates the logic of the content _____

Distinguishes between entertainment, persuasion, and factual information _____

Delivery

Evaluates the logic of the organization _____

Recognizes persuasive techniques _____

Responds constructively by questioning, challenging, or affirming _____

Recognizes the intent of the presentation _____

Evaluation Summary

Effects and the techniques used to achieve them are considered _____

Sound reasoning is used to make a judgment about the presentation _____

A conclusion regarding the presentation is reached _____

An appropriate evaluation of the presentation is made _____

Rubric for Giving and Receiving Oral Directions

Use the following rubric to evaluate giving and receiving oral directions.

Rating System

+ = excellent	✓ = average	— = weak

Receiving Directions

Focuses on the speaker _____

Visualizes the information _____

Listens for keywords _____

Takes notes or repeats aloud _____

Asks questions at the end _____

Restates the directions in own words _____

Executes all of the steps _____

Giving Directions

Focuses on the person receiving the directions _____

Proceeds step by step _____

Provides visual clues _____

Restates the directions _____

Evaluation Summary

Receiver understands the speaker's message and carries out the steps in order _____

Giver is patient and uses a step-by-step approach _____

Giver avoids adding any unnecessary details _____

Rubric for Narrative Account

Use the following rubric to evaluate narrative accounts.

Rating System

+ = excellent	✓ = average	— = weak

Content
Establishes and maintains context _____
Develops characters, setting, plot, and point of view _____
Establishes a central conflict _____
Includes sensory details and concrete language _____

Delivery
Uses appropriate verbal techniques _____
Uses appropriate nonverbal techniques _____
Presents events in chronological order _____
Exhibits a range of narrative devices _____
Appeals to background and interests of the audience _____
Achieves a focused and coherent presentation _____

Evaluation Summary
Attitude toward the topic is apparent and appropriate _____
Attitude toward the audience is apparent and appropriate _____
Preparation is evident and thorough _____
Organization is discernible and effective _____

Rubric for Presenting a Proposal

Use the following rubric to evaluate presenting a proposal.

Rating System		
+ = excellent	✓ = average	— = weak

Content

Establishes and maintains context _____
Identifies the need for action _____
States a clear position regarding a course of action _____
Arranges details, descriptions, and examples persuasively _____

Delivery

Uses appropriate verbal techniques _____
Uses appropriate nonverbal techniques _____
Organizes and presents the proposal effectively _____
Focuses on the audience _____
Addresses background and interests of the audience _____
Achieves a focused and coherent presentation _____

Presentation Summary

Attitude toward the needed action is appropriate _____
Attitude toward the audience is apparent and appropriate _____
Preparation is evident and thorough _____
Organization is discernible and effective _____

Rubric for Organizing and Delivering an Oral Summary

Use the following rubric to evaluate organizing and delivering an oral summary.

Rating System

+ = excellent	✓ = average	— = weak

Content
Establishes and maintains context _____
Briefly states main idea _____
Includes the most significant details _____
Conveys a comprehensive understanding of the source _____

Delivery
Uses appropriate verbal techniques _____
Uses appropriate nonverbal techniques _____
Organizes content _____
Addresses background and interests of the audience _____
Achieves a focused and coherent presentation _____

Presentation Summary
Attitude toward the source is apparent and appropriate _____
Attitude toward the audience is apparent and appropriate _____
Preparation is evident and thorough _____
Organization is discernible and effective _____

Rubric for Delivering a Research Presentation

Use the following rubric to evaluate research presentations.

Rating System		
+ = excellent	✓ = average	— = weak

Content
Establishes and maintains context _____
Poses a concise question on a relevant topic _____
Addresses the topic completely and thoroughly _____
Draws from multiple authoritative sources _____
Supports the topic with facts, details, examples, and explanations _____
Cites reference sources appropriately _____

Delivery
Uses appropriate verbal techniques _____
Uses appropriate nonverbal techniques _____
Uses an organizational structure that matches purpose and information _____
Presents appropriate visual aids _____
Achieves a focused and coherent presentation _____
Answers questions from the audience appropriately _____

Presentation Summary
Attitude toward topic is apparent and appropriate _____
Clear and accurate perspectives are conveyed _____
Attitude toward the audience is apparent and appropriate _____
Preparation is evident and thorough _____
Organization is discernible and effective _____

Rubric for Presenting Pros and Cons

Use the following rubric to evaluate presenting pros and cons.

Rating System		
+ = excellent	**✓ = average**	**— = weak**

Content
Establishes and maintains context _____

Poses a well-worded question _____

States each position clearly _____

Gives specific evidence for each side _____

Delivery
Uses appropriate verbal techniques _____

Uses appropriate nonverbal techniques _____

Uses an organizational structure that matches purpose and information _____

Engages the audience _____

Presents appropriate visual aids _____

Achieves a focused and coherent presentation _____

Presentation Summary
Attitude toward both sides of the topic is apparent and appropriate _____

Attitude toward the audience is apparent and appropriate _____

Preparation is evident and thorough _____

Organization is discernible and effective _____

Alternative Assessment

Name _____ Date _____

Reading Strategy Inventory

Directions: Use this inventory to help you analyze your reading habits and set goals for yourself. Think carefully about each question and answer honestly. Keep these pages for future reference. At the end of the year, you can use them to assess your progress and set new goals.

1. Which of the following strategies do you use *before* you read? Circle the word that best describes your habits.

I preview the material by thinking about
the title, reviewing any pictures, and
reading the introduction and similar
material.   never   sometimes   always

I give myself a purpose for reading,
such as deciding what I expect to learn
about the theme and how it relates to me
personally.   never   sometimes   always

I recall what I already know about
the subject about which I plan to read.   never   sometimes   always

2. Which of the following strategies do you use *while* you read? Circle the word that best describes your habits.

I try to predict what will happen and
change my prediction as I read
further.   never   sometimes   always

I ask questions about what is happening,
why characters act as they do, or why the
author chose to include particular
details or to use certain words.   never   sometimes   always

I visualize the characters and events.   never   sometimes   always

I compare characters to myself
or to people I know.   never   sometimes   always

3. Which of the following strategies do you use *after* you read? Circle the word that best describes your habits.

I respond to what I have read by
discussing it with someone.   never   sometimes   always

I review my predictions and questions
to determine if my predictions were
correct and my questions were answered.   never   sometimes   always

I use what I have learned in a
future project or activity.   never   sometimes   always

4. Put a check mark beside the responses that describe what you do when you encounter these problems. You may check more than one response. You may also add additional responses.

When I come across an unfamiliar word, I

_____ try to figure out its meaning from the way it is used.

_____ consult a dictionary.

_____ ignore it and hope it will become clear as I read further.

When I do not understand the meaning of a sentence, I

_____ read the sentence several times.

_____ read the other sentences in the paragraph several times.

_____ ignore the sentence and hope it will become clear as I read.

When I want to remember important information I have read in subjects such as science and social studies, I

_____ ask myself questions about the important ideas.

_____ relate the information to something I already know.

_____ repeat the information to myself several times.

_____ take notes.

When I read an entire passage over again, it is usually because

_____ I do not understand it.

_____ it seemed important to remember that particular passage.

_____ I want to summarize it for myself.

When reading a textbook, I

_____ read faster or slower depending on the difficulty of the material.

_____ skip parts I do not understand.

_____ make predictions about what I am reading.

When reading a textbook, I assume that

_____ all the sentences are important or they would not be there.

_____ some sentences are more important than others.

_____ sentences with the most details are the most important sentences.

Review your answers to the previous questions regarding your reading interests and strategies. Then, set goals for yourself by answering the following questions.

5. My greatest strength in reading is _____

_____

_____

_____

_____ .

6. One thing I need to improve about my reading is _____

_____

_____

_____

_____ .

7. A strategy I should use more often when reading is _____

_____

_____

_____

_____ .

8. In addition to assigned reading, I plan to read at least _____

_____

_____

_____

_____ .

9. I want to broaden my reading interests by reading more _____

_____

_____

_____

_____ .

Name _____ Date _____

Preparing to Read

Directions: Use these two sets of questions to help you prepare to read a selection and to assess the results of your reading.

Title _____ Author _____

Before I Read

1. What type of selection is this? _____

2. Why am I reading this? _____
_____

3. What do the title, pictures, and general appearance of the selection suggest about the subject or theme?
_____
_____

4. What do I know that might help me better understand this selection?
_____
_____

5. What do I know about the author and his/her style? Have I read other works by this author?
_____
_____

6. How might the theme or subject of this selection relate to my own life and experiences?
_____
_____

7. I expect this selection will provide (circle one or more)

   information   instruction   pleasure   other

   because _____.

8. I expect this to be (circle one)

   easy   average   challenging

   reading because _____.

9. What other things can I predict about the selection? What other questions do I have about it?

_____

_____

_____

After I Read

1. How accurate were my predictions or expectations? Did any questions go unanswered? Which ones?

_____

_____

_____

2. What part of the selection was the most informative or enjoyable?

_____

_____

_____

3. What part was the most troublesome or difficult?

_____

_____

_____

4. What elements provoked the strongest response? Why?

_____

_____

_____

5. What did I already know that helped me as I read?

_____

_____

_____

6. What is the most important thing I learned from reading this selection?

_____

_____

_____

Name _____ Date _____

Independent Reading Guide: The Novel

Directions: Use the following questions to clarify your understanding of and response to a novel. Reflect on each question before answering. If you are keeping a *Reader's Response Journal* or wish to start one, use one of the suggested activities to make an entry.

Novel Title _____ Author _____

Elements of the Novel

1. Who is the protagonist—the main character—in the novel?
   _____

2. What kind of person is the protagonist? _____

3. What evidence in the novel leads me to this opinion of the protagonist?
   _____

4. What challenge or conflict does the protagonist encounter? _____

5. How is the conflict resolved? _____
   _____

6. What other important characters are involved in the conflict? _____
   _____

7. What is the setting of this novel? _____

8. Who tells the story—one of the characters or an outside observer?
   _____

9. What event do I consider to be the climax of the novel? _____
   _____

10. How would I describe the mood? How does the author establish that mood?
    _____
    _____

11. State the theme or central idea of this novel. _____
    _____
    _____

12. Is there a sentence or short passage that states or strongly implies the theme? If so, what is it?

_____

_____

Response to the Novel

Rate this novel by circling the appropriate word.

13. The characters and dialogue are
believable.   weak   fair   strong

14.   The plot engages my interest. weak   fair   strong

15. This novel is written in a style that is
clear and interesting.   weak   fair   strong

16. The details in this novel add to
its appeal.   weak   fair   strong

17.   Overall, I rate this novel as   weak   fair   strong

Reasons for my rating: _____

_____

_____

18. What predictions and questions occurred to me as I read this story? Were my predictions accurate? Were my questions answered?

_____

_____

_____

_____

Reader's Response Journal

- Is there a character in this novel that you have strong feelings about? Explain your feelings. Does this character remind you of someone you know? If so, in what way? Did your feelings about this character change as the story progressed?

- Is there one event in this novel that was surprising or confusing? If so, write a brief paragraph to the author expressing your thoughts.

Independent Reading Guide: The Short Story

Directions: Use the following questions to clarify your understanding of and response to a short story. Reflect on each question before answering. If you are keeping a *Reader's Response Journal* or wish to start one, use one of the suggested activities to make an entry.

Story Title _____ Author _____

Elements of the Short Story

1. Who is the protagonist—the main character—in the story?

_____

2. What challenge or conflict does the protagonist encounter? _____

_____

3. How is the conflict resolved? _____

_____

4. What other important characters are involved in the conflict? _____

_____

5. What kind of person is the protagonist? _____

_____

6. What evidence in the story leads me to this opinion of the protagonist?

_____

_____

7. Where does this story take place? _____

_____

8. How would I describe the mood? How does the author establish this mood?

_____

_____

_____

_____

9. Summarize the theme or central idea of this short story. _____

_____

10. Is there a sentence or short passage that states or strongly implies the theme? If so, what is it?

_____

_____

Response to the Short Story

Rate this short story by circling the appropriate word.

11. The characters and dialogue are believable, and the plot engages my interest.   weak   fair   strong

12. This story is written in a style that is clear and interesting.   weak   fair   strong

13. This story helps me understand people and events.   weak   fair   strong

14. The details in this story could be easily visualized as I read.   weak   fair   strong

15. Overall, I rate this story as   weak   fair   strong

Reasons for my rating: _____

_____

_____

_____

_____

_____

_____

Reader's Response Journal

- What predictions and questions occurred to me as I read this story? Were my predictions accurate? Were my questions answered?

- In a short paragraph, describe an element of the short story that reminds you of something in your own life.

Independent Reading Guide: The Play

Directions: Use the following questions to clarify your understanding of and response to a play. Reflect on each question before answering. If you are keeping a *Reader's Response Journal* or wish to start one, use one of the suggested activities to make an entry.

Play Title _____ Author _____

Elements of the Play

1. Who is the protagonist—the main character—in the play? _____

2. What kind of person is the protagonist? _____
_____

3. What evidence in the play leads me to this opinion of the protagonist?
_____
_____

4. What challenge or conflict does the protagonist encounter? _____
_____

5. How is the conflict resolved? _____
_____
_____

6. What other important characters are involved in the conflict? _____
_____

7. Where and when does this play take place? How does the playwright reveal this information?
_____
_____

8. How would I describe the mood? How does the playwright establish this mood?
_____
_____
_____

9. Summarize the theme or central idea of this play. What other books or plays with this theme have I read?

_____

_____

10. Is there a short passage or a dialogue that states or strongly implies the theme? If so, what is it?

_____

_____

Response to the Play

Rate this play by circling the appropriate word.

11. The characters and dialogue are believable.	weak	fair	strong
12. The stage directions and the action of the characters are easily visualized.	weak	fair	strong
13. The plot of the play engages my interest.	weak	fair	strong
14. This play helps me understand people and events.	weak	fair	strong
15. This play evokes strong feelings or thoughts about the message or the characters.	weak	fair	strong
16. Reading this play increases my interest in seeing a performance of the play.	weak	fair	strong
17. Overall, I rate this play as	weak	fair	strong

Reasons for my rating: _____

_____

_____

_____

Reader's Response Journal

- What predictions and questions occurred to me as I read this play? Were my predictions accurate? Were my questions answered?

- Briefly describe a character or a scene in this play that reminds you of someone you know or an experience in your life.

Name _____ Date _____

Independent Reading Guide: Nonfiction

Directions: Use the following questions to clarify your understanding of and response to a nonfiction selection. Reflect on each question before answering. If you are keeping a *Reader's Response Journal* or wish to start one, use one of the suggested activities to make an entry.

Title _____ Author _____

Circle the type of nonfiction.

essay	biography	autobiography	sports	how-to
humor	letter	memoir	careers	astronomy
history	article	geography	personal narrative	

other _____

This nonfiction selection (circle one or more)

instructs   informs   describes   persuades   entertains.

This nonfiction selection tells about (circle one or more)

person(s)   place(s)   thing(s)   event(s)   other: _____.

Elements of Nonfiction

1. Who or what is this nonfiction selection about? _____
   _____

2. What is the author's purpose for writing this selection? _____
   _____

3. What information, facts, or examples does the author include to support the
   purpose? _____
   _____

4. For what group of people would this selection be most appealing? What does
   the author include to appeal to this audience? _____
   _____

5. What technique(s) does the author use to appeal to the reader? Circle one and
   give an example from the selection.

   description   argument   comparison and contrast

   emotional language   quotations   personal recollections

   Example: _____

6. Summarize the theme or central idea of this selection.

_____

_____

7. Is there a sentence or short passage that states or strongly implies the message or main idea? If so, what is it?

_____

_____

Response to the Nonfiction Selection

Rate this nonfiction selection by circling the appropriate word.

8. This selection is written in a style that is clear and interesting.   weak   fair   strong

9. The topic, main idea, or purpose is obvious.   weak   fair   strong

10. The details are helpful, informative, and understandable.   weak   fair   strong

11. I can connect with the author's thoughts or feelings about the subject.   weak   fair   strong

12. This selection helps me understand people and events.   weak   fair   strong

13. Overall, I rate this nonfiction selection as   weak   fair   strong

Reasons for my rating: _____

_____

14. What predictions and questions occurred to me as I read this selection? Were my predictions accurate? Were my questions answered?

_____

_____

Reader's Response Journal

- Describe something that you learned from reading this selection. Write about it and explain its significance.

- What do you think is this author's greatest strength as a writer? Write a short paragraph to explain your reason and give an example from the selection to support your reason.

Name _____ Date _____

Independent Reading Guide: Poetry

Directions: Use the following questions to clarify your understanding of and response to a poem. Reflect on each question before answering. If you are keeping a *Reader's Response Journal* or wish to start one, use one of the suggested activities to make an entry.

Poem Title _____ Poet _____

Circle the literary techniques the poet uses in this poem.

      simile   metaphor   personification   rhyme

      repetition   onomatopoeia   alliteration   other_____

In this poem, the poet is attempting to (circle one or more)

    tell a story   create an image

    express a feeling or emotion   other_____.

Elements of the Poem

1. Give an example of a literary technique used by the poet. _____

_____

2. Is the poem written in stanzas? If so, how many? _____

3. How would I describe the rhythm of the poem? _____

_____

4. Does the rhythm seem to match the message or meaning of the poem? Explain. _____

_____

_____

5. How would I describe the mood of the poem? How does the poet establish this mood? _____

_____

_____

6. What do I think the poet wants me to know, feel, value, or believe?

_____

_____

7. Does a particular word or phrase carry important meaning for the poem? If so, which word or phrase and what meaning does it convey?

_____

_____

Response to the Poem

Rate this poem by circling the appropriate word.

8. The words appeal to my sense of sight,
hearing, touch, taste, or smell.   weak   fair   strong

9. The meaning of this poem is clear
and precise.   weak   fair   strong

10. I can feel the rhythm of the poem
as I read it.   weak   fair   strong

11. I can easily connect the feelings or events
in this poem with my own experiences.   weak   fair   strong

12. Overall, I rate this poem as   weak   fair   strong

Reasons for my rating: _____

_____

13. What qualities did I like or dislike about this poem? Why? _____

_____

_____

14. What predictions and questions occurred to me as I read this poem? Were my predictions accurate? Were my questions answered?

_____

_____

Reader's Response Journal

- When you reread the poem, did you discover something that was not obvious from your first reading? Explain your discovery and the reason it may have occurred.

- Copy a phrase, line, or passage from the poem and then write a brief comment describing your feelings or thoughts about the passage.

Independent Reading Guide: Myths and Folk Tales

Directions: Use the following questions to clarify your understanding of and response to a myth, folktale, fable, or legend. Reflect on each question before answering. If you are keeping a *Reader's Response Journal* or wish to start one, use one of the suggested activities to make an entry.

Title _____ Author _____

Circle the type of selection.

        fable   myth   folk tale   legend

Circle one or more phrases that describe this selection.

       Tells about events in nature

       Explains how certain creatures came into being

       Teaches a moral lesson

       Stresses admirable behaviors or ideals

       Expresses a generalization

       Uses a symbol to stand for an idea

       Centers around a conflict

       Expresses an idea common to many people

Elements of the Myth, Folk Tale, Fable, or Legend

1. When and where does this story take place? _____
_____

2. Of what importance is the setting to the story, if any? _____
_____

3. Who are the main characters? _____

4. How would I describe the characters? What are their outstanding qualities?
_____
_____

5. What challenge or conflict do the characters encounter? _____
_____

6. How is the conflict resolved? _____
_____

7. What cultural value, belief, idea, or custom is this selection about?

_____

8. Summarize the theme, central idea, or message of this selection.

_____

9. Is there a sentence or short passage that states or strongly implies the theme, central idea, or message? If so, what is it?

_____

_____

Response to the Myth, Folk Tale, Fable, or Legend

Rate this selection by circling the appropriate word.

10. This selection is written in a style that is
clear and interesting.   weak   fair   strong

11. This selection engages my interest.   weak   fair   strong

12. The message of this selection is obvious.   weak   fair   strong

13. The message is worthwhile for today's
culture.   weak   fair   strong

14. Overall, I rate this selection as   weak   fair   strong

Reasons for my rating: _____

_____

15. Does this selection remind me of other selections I have read? If so, in

what way? _____

_____

16. What predictions and questions occurred to me as I read this story? Were my predictions accurate? Were my questions answered?

_____

_____

Reader's Response Journal

- After a careful rereading of the story, write a new ending for the story and include a new message or lesson if one is required.

- Does this story remind you of an experience or event in your life? Briefly tell how the experience relates to the story.

Initial Self-Assessment: Writing

Directions: This self-assessment is designed to help you recall the types of writing you have done, consider your strengths and weaknesses, and set goals for yourself. Answer each question or complete each statement honestly and keep it for future reference. At the end of the year, you can review this assessment and set new goals.

1. I have experience writing the following types of papers:

    _____ **Personal Expression** Expressing your thoughts, feelings, or experiences

    _____ **Description** Creating a picture of how something looks, sounds, feels, smells, or tastes

    _____ **Narration** Telling a true or fictional story

    _____ **Exposition: Giving Information** Providing information or explaining something to a reader

    _____ **Exposition: Making Connections** Comparing and contrasting, offering solutions to a problem, or explaining an opinion

    _____ **Persuasion** Trying to convince a reader to agree with you

    _____ **Reports** Summarizing the results of research

    _____ **Creative Writing** Expressing your personal views through imaginative writing like poetry

    _____ **Responses to Literature** Presenting your ideas and feelings about something you have read

2. Of the types of writing I have done, the type I am best at is _____
    _____.

3. The reasons I am good at this type of writing are _____
    _____
    _____

4. Of the types of writing I have done, the type I have the most trouble with is
    _____.

5. The reason I have trouble with this type of writing is _____
    _____.

6. I would like to try more of the following types of writing: _____
    _____.

7. I perform the following steps when I write (circle the word that applies):

Use a journal, brainstorming, or a similar method for deciding on a topic.	never	occasionally	always
Think carefully about the audience for which I am writing.	never	occasionally	always
Write down my purpose for writing before beginning a first draft.	never	occasionally	always
Write a draft without stopping to correct spelling and mechanical problems.	never	occasionally	always
Ask someone else to read my draft before revising.	never	occasionally	always
Proofread and correct mechanical spelling errors after the draft has been revised.	never	occasionally	always
Try to make my final copy neat and attractive.	never	occasionally	always

8. The step in the writing process I do best is _____

_____

_____

_____

9. The reason I am particularly good at this is _____

_____

_____

_____

10. The best thing about my writing is _____

_____

_____

_____

11. The step in the writing process I most need to improve is _____

_____

_____

_____

12. I need to work on this because _____

_____

_____

_____

Name _____ Date _____

Peer Conferencing Notes: Reader

Directions: Read your classmate's draft and make suggestions for improvement. Remember that your classmate needs specific suggestions. Ask yourself one or more of these questions, make notes on your answers, and share your answers with the writer.

Name of Writer _____ Date _____

Name of Reviewer _____ Date _____

1. What do you see as the writer's purpose? Is it clear?

   _____

   _____

   _____

2. Is the topic too broad/too narrow to cover in a paper like this? If so, how should the writer narrow/broaden the topic?

   _____

   _____

   _____

3. Does the beginning make me want to read the rest of the paper? If not, why?

   _____

   _____

   _____

4. Are there places where you wish the writer had included more information? If so, where?

   _____

   _____

   _____

5. Are there parts that could be left out? What are they?

   _____

   _____

6. Are there places where the writer could have used more exact or appropriate words? What words do you suggest?

   _____

   _____

7. Are the ideas presented logically and are they easy to follow? Are there any parts you found confusing? If so, what parts?

_____

_____

8. What could the writer do to make the paper easier to follow?

_____

_____

_____

9. What do you like best about the paper? Why?

_____

_____

_____

_____

_____

_____

_____

10. What one thing could the writer do to most improve this paper?

_____

_____

_____

Proofreading Checklist

Directions: Use this checklist to review the grammar, usage, mechanics, and s pelling before presenting your work. You may want to use the proofreading symbols shown here to mark your draft. It is usually best to first make any revisions in organization, detail, transitions, and similar elements.

Proofreading Marks

∧	Insert a letter or word here.	#	Insert a space here.
(n\t)	Switch the order of two letters or words.	¶	Begin a new paragraph.
⁄X	Make this letter lowercase.	≝	Capitalize this letter.
‿	Link inserted material.	∧	Add a comma.
⌄⌄	Add quotation marks.	⊙	Add a period.
ℰ	Take out a word, sentence, or punctuation mark.		

Grammar and Usage

_____ Do the subjects and verbs in my sentences agree?

_____ Did I use complete sentences?

_____ Did I incorrectly run any sentences together without proper punctuation? Have I corrected them?

_____ Did I use the correct form of irregular verbs?

_____ Did I indent the first line of each paragraph?

_____ Did I use the correct form of personal pronouns?

_____ Did I use adjectives and adverbs correctly in comparisons?

_____ Did I use any double negatives? If so, did I correct them?

Punctuation and Capitalization

_____ Did I end each sentence with the correct punctuation?

_____ Did I use commas and semicolons correctly?

_____ Did I capitalize all proper nouns correctly, including names of characters, nicknames, and place names?

_____ Did I begin each sentence or direct quotation with a capital letter?

_____ Did I use quotation marks to show the beginning and end of another's exact words?

_____ Did I use apostrophes where needed to show possession or missing letters?

Spelling

_____ Did I check the spelling of the names of people and places?

_____ Did I use the correct form of words that sound alike but have different spellings and meanings?

_____ Did I check the spelling of words I am not sure of, especially troublesome words like _their_ and _there_?

Organization

_____ Did I make my thesis clear?

_____ Does each paragraph contain a topic sentence?

_____ Did I make sure that the topic sentences support my thesis?

_____ Did I elaborate on my main ideas?

_____ Did I pull everything together in a strong conclusion?

Name _____ Date _____

Writing Self-Assessement

Directions: These questions will help you review the process you used to write a paper. The best time to use this is immediately after you have published or presented the final version, while the experience is still fresh in your mind. You may wish to review your answers to these questions before you write your next paper.

Title of Paper _____

Type of Writing _____

Date Begun _____ Date Completed _____

1. I used the following strategy for choosing and narrowing my topic:

   _____

   _____

2. How successful was this strategy? Would I use it again? How would I change it the next time?

   _____

   _____

3. How did I gather information for this paper? Was this an efficient and productive method? What other method might I have used?

   _____

   _____

4. How did I decide on the organization for the information I gathered? Was this a good strategy for making that decision? Are there other strategies that might have worked better?

   _____

   _____

5. The prewriting activities that helped me the most when writing the draft were

   _____

   _____.

6. In revising and editing my draft I tried to focus on _____

   _____

   _____

   _____.

7. One strategy I used in revising that helped was _____

_____

_____ .

8. One strategy I wish I had tried is _____

_____

_____ .

9. In proofreading for grammar, usage, mechanics, and spelling errors, I need to pay more attention to

_____

_____

_____ .

10. The thing I did most successfully in this paper was _____

_____

_____

_____ .

11. The thing I most need to work on in my next paper is _____

_____

_____

_____ .

12. The next time I write a paper of this type, I want to be sure to remember

_____

_____

_____ .

Portfolio Planner

Directions: Use this form to record and clarify the goals of your portfolio and to identify the strategies and resources you expect to use in pursuing those goals. Keep a copy of this planner handy to track your progress and record notes from conferences with your teacher. When your portfolio is complete, use this form in conjunction with the Portfolio Self-Evaluation form to assess how well you did.

Part I: Goals

1. Type of portfolio:

_____ Working Portfolio to collect and organize work in progress

_____ Presentation Portfolio to showcase my best work

_____ Other _____

2. My specific goal for this portfolio is _____

_____

_____

_____.

3. To achieve this goal, I will need to focus on developing the following skills:

_____

_____

_____

4. The finished portfolio will show the following things about me:

_____

_____

_____

5. The finished portfolio will demonstrate the following strengths and abilities:

_____

_____

_____

Part II: Strategies and Resources

6. I will need to do these assignments and activities to reach my goals:

_____

_____

_____

7. I expect to complete this portfolio by _____.

8. Complete the following chart to plan the specific steps in completing your portfolio. As you complete each step, record the date in the last column.

Goal:

Step	Task: Assignment or Activity	Materials and Resources Needed	Will Be Completed By	Date Completed
1.				
2.				
3.				
4.				
5.				
6.				
7.				
8.				

Plan Approval

Date of Conference _____ Teacher's Signature _____

Suggestions _____

Progress Check

Date of Conference _____ Teacher's Signature _____

Suggestions _____

Date of Conference _____ Teacher's Signature _____

Suggestions _____

Name _____ Date _____

Portfolio Record

Directions: Use this form to record and update information about the writing you place in your portfolio. You may want to attach this form to the cover of your portfolio so it serves as a reminder to record all contents. Your teacher may ask you to keep a portfolio for a particular unit of study. If so, indicate the unit represented by this portfolio.

Unit _____

Title of Paper _____

Stage of Development:　　　Prewriting　　　　　　Date _____

　　　　　　　　　　　　　　　Drafting　　　　　　　Date _____

　　　　　　　　　　　　　　　Revising and Editing　Date _____

　　　　　　　　　　　　　　　Finished Paper　　　　Date _____

Title of Paper _____

Stage of Development:　　　Prewriting　　　　　　Date _____

　　　　　　　　　　　　　　　Drafting　　　　　　　Date _____

　　　　　　　　　　　　　　　Revising and Editing　Date _____

　　　　　　　　　　　　　　　Finished Paper　　　　Date _____

Title of Paper _____

Stage of Development:　　　Prewriting　　　　　　Date _____

　　　　　　　　　　　　　　　Drafting　　　　　　　Date _____

　　　　　　　　　　　　　　　Revising and Editing　Date _____

　　　　　　　　　　　　　　　Finished Paper　　　　Date _____

Title of Paper _____

Stage of Development:　　　Prewriting　　　　　　Date _____

　　　　　　　　　　　　　　　Drafting　　　　　　　Date _____

　　　　　　　　　　　　　　　Revising and Editing　Date _____

　　　　　　　　　　　　　　　Finished Paper　　　　Date _____

Title of Paper _____

Stage of Development: Prewriting   Date _____

                         Drafting   Date _____

                         Revising and Editing   Date _____

                         Finished Paper   Date _____

Title of Paper _____

Stage of Development: Prewriting   Date _____

                         Drafting   Date _____

                         Revising and Editing   Date _____

                         Finished Paper   Date _____

Title of Paper _____

Stage of Development: Prewriting   Date _____

                         Drafting   Date _____

                         Revising and Editing   Date _____

                         Finished Paper   Date _____

Title of Paper _____

Stage of Development: Prewriting   Date _____

                         Drafting   Date _____

                         Revising and Editing   Date _____

                         Finished Paper   Date _____

Title of Paper _____

Stage of Development: Prewriting   Date _____

                         Drafting   Date _____

                         Revising and Editing   Date _____

                         Finished Paper   Date _____

Name _____ Date _____

Portfolio Final Self-Evaluation

Directions: This evaluation form will help you assess your completed portfolio. Review the contents of your portfolio and answer the following questions to see which goals you have met and which goals you need to continue working toward.

1. Does your completed portfolio meet the goals you set for this unit? _____ If your answer is yes, list the items you feel fulfill the goals and explain your choices. If your answer is no, tell why.

   _____

   _____

   _____

   _____

2. Does your completed portfolio satisfactorily demonstrate the strengths and abilities you specified? _____ If your answer is yes, list the items and tell how they demonstrate the strength or ability. If your answer is no, explain why you are not satisfied that this strength or ability has been demonstrated.

   _____

   _____

   _____

3. Which step in your planning chart was completed most successfully? What made this step successful? Which step proved to be the most difficult? What made this step difficult?

   _____

   _____

   _____

4. The best thing about the work in this portfolio is _____

   _____

   _____.

5. The most important thing I learned in completing this portfolio is _____

   _____

   _____.

6. The thing I am least satisfied about in this portfolio is _____

   _____.

7. A goal for my next portfolio will be _____

   _____.

Portfolio Final Evaluation: Teacher Rating

Directions: Use this form for an overall assessment of the completed student portfolio. In addition, you may ask the student to complete a Portfolio Final Self-Evaluation form. These forms can be placed in the portfolio and referred to during student or parent conferences.

I. Assessment of Individual Items

Rate each item in the portfolio from 1 to 4, with 4 being the highest.

Item and Goal	Rating	Comments

II. Overall Assessment

Rate the overall achievement of the portfolio in these areas using the following rubrics:

_____ Focus

    4. All items reflect a clear sense of goals and a focused strategy for attaining them.

    3. Most items reflect the stated goals of the portfolios, but work includes a few unproductive strategies.

    2. Goals are lacking in clarity, and strategies have regular lapses in focus.

    1. No consistent goal and generally aimless activities in this portfolio.

_____ Variety

4. Items are highly varied and demonstrate competence and creativity in many areas.

3. Items reflect some variety and demonstrate competence and creativity in several areas.

2. Items are generally of one type with some new competencies and/or occasional creativity.

1. Items are of one type and show little or no concern for originality.

_____ Attitude

4. Shows enthusiasm for and commitment to achieving stated goals.

3. Generally positive about achieving stated goals but shows occasional periods of inactivity or low interest.

2. Needs regular urging or reminders to complete steps in the portfolio plan.

1. Completely lacking in enthusiasm and commitment; works on portfolio only after repeated reminders.

_____ Progress

4. Portfolio shows substantial progress over previous work in a broad range of skills and competencies.

3. Measurable growth and progress in several areas of skills and competencies.

2. Modest growth and progress in one or two areas.

1. No noticeable growth in any area; work is mechanical and repetitious.

Additional observations: _____

_____

_____

The best work in the portfolio is _____.

An area needing further attention is _____

_____

_____.

Some goals for the next portfolio should be _____

_____

_____.

Evaluator's Signature _____

Date _____

Self-Assessment: Speech

Directions: When you speak before a group, your goal is to present information to your listeners in an interesting way. When you give a speech, you usually want your words to persuade listeners to believe or do something. Use this sheet to evaluate your speaking techniques and to assess your ability to compose and deliver an effective speech.

Circle the word that best applies to your speaking habits and techniques.

1. I look forward to speaking before a group.   never   occasionally always

2. I plan what I am going to say before I   never   occasionally always
begin to speak.

3. I speak in a clear, confident voice.   never   occasionally always

4. I use language and gestures that are   never   occasionally always
appropriate to the occasion, audience,
and purpose.

5. I engage listeners by making eye contact.   never   occasionally always

6. When I have to give a speech, I prepare in the following ways:

_____ I do the necessary research to speak intelligently on my topic.

_____ I consider my audience and purpose when choosing anecdotes, facts,
details, and quotes to include in my speech.

_____ I organize my ideas in a way that will be clear to follow.

_____ I decide on an appropriate opening statement, quotation, joke, or
anecdote that will hook listeners.

_____ I rehearse my speech to improve my performance.

7. I recently gave a speech on _____

_____.

8. The best part of my speech was _____

_____.

9. The part that listeners seemed to like the best was _____

_____.

10. If I were to give that speech again, I would make it better by _____

_____.

Name _____ Date _____

Peer Assessment: Speech

Directions: Use this sheet to assess a speech given by one of your classmates. Be honest but keep in mind that harsh, critical comments can be hurtful. Your goal is to help your classmate recognize the successful elements of his or her speech as well as areas that need improvement.

Name of Speaker: _____

Topic: _____

_____ Assigned by Teacher   _____ Chosen by Student

	Point Scale	
Rate the speaker according to the following scale. Write the matching number in the space.	4 = Thoroughly	2 = Very little
	3 = Mostly	1 = Not at all

_____ **1.** The speaker prepared for this speech.

_____ **2.** The speaker was relaxed and confident.

_____ **3.** The speaker spoke clearly and slowly.

_____ **4.** The speaker made eye contact with listeners.

_____ **5.** The speaker used appropriate gestures and facial expressions.

_____ **6.** The speaker used graphic aids effectively.

Use your own words to assess each element of the speech:

Introduction _____

_____

Body _____

_____

Conclusion _____

_____

Organization of Ideas _____

_____

_____

Sentence Variety _____

_____

Level of Interest _____

_____

Name _____ Date _____

Peer Assessment: Oral Interpretation

Directions: A successful oral interpretation communicates the message of a piece of literature. Read the guidelines for a successful presentation of an oral interpretation and use them in two ways:

1. Follow them as you prepare an oral interpretation.

2. Use them to evaluate others' interpretations.

As you listen to a classmate's oral interpretation, write your assessment of how the speaker meets each guideline.

Speaker's Name _____

The oral reading was taken from _____ .

Oral Interpretation Guidelines	Your Assessment of the Speaker
1. The piece of literature is selected with the audience and a specific purpose in mind. The time allowed for the presentation is considered.	
2. The work is cut, but the order of the story events still remains clear. Speech tags (*she smiled*) that can be presented through body language can be cut. Passages that do not contribute to the dramatic effect the speaker hopes to achieve can also be cut or trimmed.	
3. The introduction gives the title and author of the work and sets the scene for the part of the story that will be read. Any important events that took place earlier in the story are included.	
4. The speaker uses his or her face, body, and voice (volume, pitch, tone, pronunciation, speed) to build drama, bring the characters to life, and create an overall impression.	
5. The speaker allows the audience time to react to humorous, surprising, sad, or other emotional parts of the reading.	

Name _____ Date _____

Peer Assessment: Dramatic Performance

Directions: You may have an opportunity to watch two or three of your classmates give a short dramatic performance. Use this sheet to evaluate their performance. Answer each question as thoroughly and as honestly as you can.

1. Who participated in the performance? _____

2. What work did they perform? _____

3. How appropriate was the work for the audience? _____
   _____

4. How prepared were the student performers? Did they know their lines?
   _____
   _____

5. Were the movements, gestures, and facial expressions appropriate to the work? Explain.
   _____
   _____

6. How well could you hear the performers? Why do you think this was so?
   _____
   _____

7. Did the performers make use of any props during the performance? In what way did they enhance or detract from the performance?
   _____
   _____

8. How did the audience react? _____

9. Overall, I think this performance was _____
   _____

10. If students have a chance to perform this work again, I would suggest they
    _____
    _____

Name _____ Date _____

Self-Assessment: Listening

Directions: Active listening is an important part of the learning experience. Use this sheet when you listen in school to help you evaluate your success as an active listener.

Put a check mark next to each statement that applies to you.

Listening Skills	Always	Sometimes	Seldom	Never
1. I am relaxed and attentive.				
2. I determine the speaker's purpose and my purpose for listening.				
3. I think about what the speaker is saying and recognize the main points.				
4. I am polite. I do not interrupt or cause any kind of disturbance.				
5. I concentrate on the words, especially toward the middle of the presentation when I might tend to become distracted.				
6. I ask questions whenever I do not understand something.				
7. I take notes when appropriate.				
8. At the end of an oral presentation, I mentally summarize what I have heard.				
9. In a discussion, I allow others the chance to speak.				
10. In a discussion, I listen carefully to a speaker so that I can respond appropriately.				

11. What do you think are the most important traits of an active listener?

_____   _____

_____   _____

12. Which of the traits that you listed is your strongest? Which is your weakest? What can you do to improve that trait to become a better listener?

_____

_____

General Resources

Name _____ Date _____

Self-Assessment: Speaking and Listening Progress

Directions: This page is designed to help you track your speaking and listening progress. This chart will give you insight into your average daily speaking and listening opportunities.

Rating Key   E = Excellent   G = Good   S = Satisfactory   NI = Needs Improvement

Date	Place	Speaking/Listening	Describe What Happened	Rating

Name _____

Date _____

Speaking Progress Chart: Teacher Observation

Directions: This chart is designed to help you assess your students' speaking behavior. Write the students' names in the first column. Use the key to record your observations for each behavior. Share your observations with students to help them recognize their speaking skills and to help them set goals for improving.

Key   **P** = Proficient   **I** = Improving   **N** = Needs Attention

Student's Name	Speaks clearly and loudly.	Appears calm and confident.	Is prepared and knows material.	Uses body language and gestures effectively.	Uses visual aids effectively.

Name _____ Date _____

Teacher Observation Checklist

Directions: This instrument is designed to help you identify and record behavior related to future job performance. It has been derived from a report by the Secretary's Commission on Achieving Necessary Skills (SCANS) published by the Department of Labor. In the center column, write a brief description of the behavior observed and the date and circumstances of the observation. In the right column indicate the level of readiness you assess this behavior demonstrates: **P** for Preparatory, **W** for Work Ready, and **A** for Advanced. Add to this log periodically throughout the school year.

I. Basic Skills: Reading	Behavior	Level of Readiness
1. Locates, understands, and interprets written information from text, graphs, or schedules to perform a task.		
2. Identifies the main idea or essential message in written text.		
3. Infers relevant details, facts, and specifications.		
4. Uses contextual clues or finds meaning for unknown or technical vocabulary.		
5. Judges the accuracy, appropriateness, style, and plausibility of reports or proposals of other writers.		
II. Basic Skills: Writing		
6. Records information completely and accurately.		
7. Uses graphs and flowcharts to present information.		
8. Uses language, style, organization, and format appropriate to the subject matter, purpose, and audience.		
9. Includes supporting documentation.		
10. Uses appropriate level of detail.		
11. Checks, edits, and revises for correct information, appropriate emphasis, and form.		
12. Checks, edits, and revises for correct grammar, spelling, and punctuation.		

III. Basic Skills: Listening	Behavior	Level of Readiness
13. Critically evalutates a verbal message.		
14. Responds appropriately to a verbal message.		
15. Critically evaluates nonverbal messages, such as body language.		
16. Responds appropriately to a nonverbal message.		
IV. Basic Skills: Speaking		
17. Communicates oral messages appropriate to listeners and situations.		
18. Makes a positive contribution to conversations and discussions.		
19. Makes a positive contribution to a group presentation.		
20. Selects an appropriate medium for conveying a message.		
21. Uses language appropriate in style, tone, and level of complexity to the audience, the message, and the occasion.		
22. Uses body language appropriate to the audience, the message, and the occasion.		
23. Articulates a message clearly and confidently.		
24. Understands and responds to listener feedback.		
25. Asks questions when needed.		
V. Thinking Skills: Creative Thinking		
26. Uses imagination freely.		
27. Combines information in new ways.		
28. Makes connections between seemingly unrelated ideas.		
29. Revises goals in ways that reveal new possibilities.		

VI. Thinking Skills: Decision Making	Behavior	Level of Readiness
30. Specifies goals and limitations.		
31. Generates alternatives.		
32. Considers risks.		
33. Evaluates and chooses best alternatives.		
VII. Thinking Skills: Problem Solving		
34. Recognizes that a problem exists (i.e., identifies a discrepancy between what is and what should or could be).		
35. Identifies possible reasons for discrepancy.		
36. Devises and implements a plan to resolve discrepancy.		
37. Evaluates and monitors progress of the resolution.		
38. Revises plan as indicated by findings.		
VIII. Thinking Skills: Reasoning		
39. Uses logic to draw conclusions from available information.		
40. Extracts rules or principles from a set of objects or written text.		
41. Applies rules and principles to a new situation.		
42. Determines which conclusions are correct when given a set of facts and a set of conclusions.		

General Resources

Date _____

Dear Parent or Guardian,

Recent studies show how important parental involvement is in helping students achieve success in school. Because I know that you want your child to have an excellent year in English, I am pleased to tell you about our curriculum and suggest some ways you can participate in improving your child's performance.

In English this year we will be using *Prentice Hall Literature: Penguin Edition*. This program combines a wide variety of quality reading selections with literature analysis, critical thinking and reading skills, and composition. Importantly, it connects the literature to students' own experiences through the development of themes relevant to students' lives.

You can help your child get the most from this program and from all of his or her homework by following this expert-tested advice.

- **Find the best time for studying.** Work with your child to decide on the best time for studying. Then set that time aside at least five days out of every week. If there is no homework, your child can use the time to review or plan ahead.

- **Eliminate common distractions.** Set aside a study area that is free from noise and other distractions. Turn off the TV. Your child may say that watching television is helpful, but no research supports this. In fact, watching television allows students to turn off their minds because it requires no action or interaction.

- **Avoid common interruptions.** Take messages if the telephone rings and have your child alert his or her friends not to drop by during the established study time.

- **Provide physical conditions that help concentration.** Ensure that the study area has adequate lighting and is kept at a comfortable temperature. Provide a table or desk that has enough space for writing.

- **Keep supplies handy.** Keeping studying materials nearby saves time. Placing them in a small bucket or box makes it easy to move them to the study area. A list of supplies should also include a dictionary and a thesaurus.

- **Encourage computer literacy.** Help your child to see the value of using the computer to write his or her compositions and other assignments. Encourage your child to use the computers at school or the public library. If you have a home computer, provide quality word-processing software for your child.

- **Ask to see your child's books.** Looking through the books gives you a better idea of what your child is learning and shows him or her that you think the material is important.

- **Ask to see your child's work on a regular basis.** You do not need to criticize or regrade the papers. That will only make your child less willing to show you his or her work. Just let your child know you are interested.

- **Read.** By watching you read, your child will see reading as a valuable activity. You can be especially effective if you occasionally read and discuss one of the selections your child is covering in class.

I look forward to working with your child and hope you will contact me if you have any questions during the school year.

Cordially,

_____

English Teacher

Name _____ Date _____

Self-Assessment: Home Review

Directions: Fill in the name of an adult friend or family member on the line below and attach the completed *Initial Self-Assessment*. Plan to spend some time discussing your writing with this person. You will not be asked to turn in this page. It is entirely between you and your friend or family member.

Dear _____,

    We are about to begin our work in writing at school. I used the attached self-assessment page to help me think about the types of writing I have done, to examine how I go about the task of writing, to analyze my strengths and weaknesses, and to set goals for the year.

    I would appreciate if you would look over my answers and goals and review them with me from time to time. I will share some of the things I write in school with you so we can both follow my progress.

    In addition, I would be interested in knowing something about your experiences with writing. For example,

1. What kinds of writing have you had to do? How important was it that you wrote well in those situations?

2. How and where did you learn to write?

3. What are your strengths and weaknesses as a writer?

4. Do you think writing will always be an important skill? Why?

_____

_____

_____

_____

_____

                              Sincerely,

                              _____

Name _____ Date _____

Homework Log

Directions: Use this homework log to keep track of your daily assignments. After completing each assignment, have a parent or guardian look over your work and sign the log.

Subject and Assignment	Date Due	Date Completed	Parent/Guardian Signature

Name _____ Date _____

Writing: Home Review Letter

To the Student: Fill in the name of a family member or an adult friend and attach this letter to the final version of your work to request comments on your work.

Date _____

Dear _____,

    I am attaching something that I wrote in school recently. I would appreciate it if you would read it and tell me what you think of it. I am particularly interested in getting your answers to the questions below. You can answer them on the lines under each question.

What do you think my purpose is for writing this?

_____

Were you able to follow my thoughts? If not, where did you get lost? What could I have done to make it easier to follow along?

_____

Is there any information you wish I had included? If so, what?

_____

_____

Are there any parts you think I could have left out? If so, which parts?

_____

_____

What do you like best about what I have written?

_____

_____

What else would you like to tell me about what I have written?

_____

_____

    Thank you for your help.

Sincerely yours,

_____

Writing Student